PROCLAIMING THE NEW TESTAMENT

The Gospel of Luke

PROCLAIMING THE NEW TESTAMENT

The Gospel
of Luke

by
Ralph Earle

BAKER BOOK HOUSE
Grand Rapids, Michigan

Library of Congress Catalog Card Number: 68-14968

PHOTOLITHOPRINTED BY CUSHING - MALLOY, INC.
ANN ARBOR, MICHIGAN, UNITED STATES OF AMERICA
1 9 6 7

Editor's Foreword

In the series, Proclaiming the New Testament, an attempt is made to provide homiletical comments and ideas. The busy pastor needs to spend time in meditation if he is to offer the bread of life to his people. One of the best known methods of Bible study is to work through one book of the Bible at a time. This gives depth as well as breadth. It provides for the preaching of the whole counsel of God and not just a part of that revelation. As truth must reach people in various stages of growth and at different levels of reception, so there must be variety of communication.

The intention of this series is to stimulate men in the ministry to more definite study. Believing that the first rule of homiletics is to read and study the actual text of Scripture, this method brings ideas and suggestion. Here illustrations are limited as the individual should find his own as he reads or mingles with people, and as he is open to all the winds of God. No pastor can lead his people to a level of thought and spiritual experience higher than the one he occupies. God will not honor lazy men or men who imagine the Holy Spirit should prompt alone. God has given us a mind to use, a heart to love, a spirit to pray, and a will to study.

These results are possible from this approach. *One,* the pastor and student will find suggestive ideas. As Charles H. Spurgeon said of William Gurnall (1616-79), a Puritan, "I have found his work the best thought-breeder in all our library. I should think more discourses have been suggested by it than by any other. I have often resorted to it when my own fire has been burning low. . . ." *Two,* the user will see how to study an entire book of the Bible for preaching values. *Three,* the man of God will be encouraged to begin the study of the Bible book for himself and find by this method other treasures of homiletical insight.

While using the King James or Authorized Version, the student should compare with all other versions and translations as well as the original text when available.

5

Many and varied are the commentaries available for the profit of the preacher. These include the following:

I. *Critical.* This deals with the text in the light of biblical criticism, seeking to apply historical principles and a rational approach to the text, e.g., *The International Critical Commentary, the Moffatt New Testament Commentary, The Expositor's Greek Testament,* and the commentaries of H. A. W. Meyer, and Keil and Delitsch.

II. *Exegetical.* This seeks to lead out the exact meaning of the text in terms of the words and idioms in the light of their background and use originally, e.g., *The Westminster Commentaries, the New International Commentary on the New Testament, The Evangelical Commentary on the New Testament,* and the commentaries of R. C. H. Lenski, J. P. Lange, and W. Hendriksen.

III. *Expository.* This expounds and applies the dominant theme of each section or unit in the light of history and with relevance to the present, e.g., *The Expositor's Bible, The Interpreter's Bible, Calvin's Commentaries, The Pulpit Commentary,* and *An American Commentary on the New Testament.*

IV. *Devotional.* This brings out the inner sense or the spiritual essence as applied to the soul in meditation. Here is the stimulus to the spiritual life of the believer, e.g., *A Devotional Commentary,* and Matthew Henry's *Commentary on the Whole Bible.*

The present type of book is neither a Bible study book nor a book of outlines. It is not a commentary as the above. We seek to encourage the preacher to engage in the reading and studying of the book to find the homiletical units. As "the servant of the Word" let him work toward this ideal:

the Historical setting,
the Expository meaning,
the Doctrinal value,
the Practical aim,
the Homiletical form

The First Presbyterian Church
of Seattle, Washington

Ralph G. Turnbull
General Editor

Author's Introduction

"The most beautiful book ever written." That was how Renan described the Gospel of Luke.

It has special human interest appeal. The personality of Luke shows through very clearly. He was an unusually gracious Christian gentleman. Probably he was the most widely read and most widely traveled man in the first century church. It is generally held that he was the single Gentile writer of Scripture. He wrote two of the twenty-seven books of the New Testament — the third Gospel and Acts. But they are the two longest and together they comprise more than one fourth of the total contents.

Luke was the friend of the underdog. He was the champion of the rights of the Gentiles, of the Samaritans, of women, of children, of the poor, of sinners, of outcasts. In a day when social justice is being strongly advocated, Luke has something to say to us.

Most of the best known parables, the all-time favorites, are found only in Luke. One only need enumerate a few: the Good Samaritan, the Prodigal Son, the Unjust Steward, the Rich Fool.

Luke was evidently a great man of prayer. This is shown by the fact that he gives more attention to prayer than do any of the other Gospel writers. He does this in two ways. First, he mentions Jesus as praying on six different occasions (e.g., at His baptism and transfiguration) where the other Gospels omit this feature. Secondly, he gives more of Jesus' teachings on prayers. He alone preserves for us the three great parables on prayer: the Importunate Friend at Midnight, the Importunate Widow (or Unjust Judge), and the Pharisee and the Publican. These are found in the eleventh and eighteenth chapters.

Luke presents Jesus as the Son of Man. He gives such beautiful domestic touches as the unforgettable picture of

7

Martha and Mary (10:38-42), of Jesus and the two disciples
from Emmaus (24:13-35). Luke was an artist with words.
There is an ancient tradition that he was a painter of pic-
tures. He loved poetry. Paul calls him "the beloved physician" (Col. 4:14). He was a great soul. His Gospel can be
rich resource for preaching.

Contents

Luke 1

SERVICE THAT IS SACRED

1:74-75. "That he would grant unto us, that we being delivered out of the hand of our enemies might serve him without fear, in holiness and righteousness before him, all the days of our life."

I. HISTORICAL SETTING. Luke was a great historian. After a brief Preface of four verses — a gem of classical Greek — he begins his Gospel proper at 1:5. Typically, his opening words are: "There was in the days of Herod, the king of Judaea." This was Herod the Great, who ruled Palestine 37-4 B.C. He was an Idumaean (Edomite) with some Jewish blood in his veins. The incident recorded here probably took place in 6 B.C., something over a year before Jesus was born in 5 B.C.

II. EXPOSITORY MEANING. The word for "delivered" basically means "rescued." Christ was to come to rescue people from the clutches of sin and Satan. Thus delivered, they are to serve their Deliverer.

Four different Greek verbs are translated "serve" in the King James Version of the New Testament. The one here is *latreuo*. It may also be translated "worship." Actually true worship is the primary element in acceptable service to God.

The Greek word for "holiness" is a rare one, found only here and in Ephesians 4:24. In both places it is associated with "righteousness." The essential meaning of *hosiotes* is "piety," or a devout attitude toward God. Cremer says that "it denotes the spirit and conduct of one who is joined in fellowship with God."

"Righteousness" is a very common word in the New Testament, occurring 100 times (41 times in Romans). The Greek word used here is *dikaiosyne*. Thayer gives this definition:

11

"integrity, virtue, purity of life, uprightness, correctness in thinking, feeling, and acting." Of *dikaiosyne* and *hosiotes* he says that "the former denotes right conduct toward men, the latter piety towards God."

III. DOCTRINAL VALUE. Redemption is the keynote here (cf. 1:68). God has bought back his people, ransomed them from the slavery of sin. This involves remission of sins, which brings to one salvation (1:77). The "dayspring" (dawn) had appeared, "to give light to them that sit in darkness" and to "guide . . . into the way of peace" (1:78-79). This is what salvation does for the one who responds to the light of God's love.

The material here is naturally couched in Old Testament language, for Zechariah properly belongs to the old dispensation. But he spoke better than he knew. He was prophesying under the inspiration of the Spirit (1:67) and so predicted the salvation which would be provided in the great Deliverer, Jesus Christ. The Old Testament prophecies were being fulfilled in the coming of the Messiah.

IV. PRACTICAL AIM. The purpose of this passage is to show that salvation does not come through our own efforts but by a divine deliverance. No man can save himself. All men must look to God and trust only in Him if they would be saved.

V. HOMILETICAL FORM

Theme: "Service That Is Sacred."

Introduction: What the Jews wanted was political salvation, deliverance from domination by Rome. What they needed was personal salvation, deliverance from the dominion of sin.

So it is today. Modern society is crying out for reformation — racial, social, economic, political. What it desperately needs is regeneration, a spiritual renewal.

The central theme of Zechariah's Benedictus (1:68-79) is salvation. This means the forgiveness of sins and the living of a holy life. We are to be saved, not *in* sin but *from* sin. Purity must precede peace. Christ brings both.

The service that is sacred is:

A. *Service without Fear*

We are saved by faith. But faith banishes fear. The trusting soul is not afraid.

Paul wrote to Timothy: "For God hath not given us the spirit of fear; but of power, and of love, and of a sound mind" (II Tim. 1:7). The fearful saint cannot serve God either acceptably or effectively.

The secret of forever banishing fear is to realize that we are "in Christ." In Him we are delivered from our great enemy, sin. In Him we are protected against the onslaughts of Satan. In Him we have peace and purity and power. Apart from Him we have none of these.

Fear is a denial of faith. God does not want His children to live in fear. Peter walking on the water was all right as long as he looked at Jesus. But when he let his eyes drop to his surrounding circumstances he was terrified and began to sink. And so shall we. But Jesus is right there to rescue us, as He did Peter.

B. *Service in Holiness*

Holiness has to do primarily with our relationship to God. This is primary. What we are is more important than what we do. Inner piety must precede and produce outward performance. We cannot live a righteous life before our fellow men unless we maintain a holy fellowship in our hearts with God.

The trouble with most modern religion is that it starts with the outside of man, rather than the inside. In fact, one prominent writer in the field of psychology of religion has defined religion as "the sum total of human relationships."

When humanism gets rid of God it has to deny the reality of sin. There is no sin and no Savior. But this is a far cry from the religion of the Bible. It begins with God, shows man guilty and enslaved to sin, and then presents the Savior.

Only with holy hearts can we serve God acceptably. But He must make us holy.

C. Service in Righteousness

While the vertical relationships of life are all-important, the horizontal ones are also important. We cannot retain our right relationship to God unless we continually maintain a right relationship to our fellow men. That is the main thrust of Hebrews 12:14, which literally reads: "Keep on pursuing peace with all men and the sanctification apart from which no one shall see the Lord."

That is why we need to meet God in the morning before we meet men all day. We need the inner touch of Christ if we are going to live the Christian life.

We cannot be right with our fellow men unless we are first right with God. Inward holiness of heart must precede outward righteousness of life. We need to be sure that we are "in Christ" — not only positionally but powerfully — when we meet men. They must be confronted with Christ in us.

Luke 2

GOD'S GLORY AND MAN'S GOOD

2:14. "Glory to God in the highest, and on earth peace, good will toward men."

I. HISTORICAL SETTING. We do not know with certainty the exact day, month, or year in which Jesus was born. Because it is said that the shepherds were "abiding in the field, keeping watch over their flock by night" (v. 8), some have claimed this could not have been in late December. So October has been suggested as a substitute. But Samuel Andrews (*Life of Our Lord*, p. 16) writes that there is "no good ground to affirm that shepherds could not have been pasturing their flocks in the field during the month of December."

What about the year? In the sixth century a man named Dionysius figured the time of Christ's birth, and his system of dating events A.D. became common during the reign of Charlemagne (ninth century). But we know now that Dionysius was at least four years off in his calculation. For Herod the Great died in 4 B.C., and he was ruling when Jesus was born (Matt. 2:1). It is generally agreed today that Christ was born at least as early as 5 B.C., and possible in 6 B.C. Palestine was under Roman rule.

II. EXPOSITORY MEANING. The word for "glory" (*doxa*) may be translated "praise" or "honor." It is stated that the angelic host was "praising God" (v. 13).

The Greek begins: "Glory in the highest to God." The literal Latin of this, *Gloria in Excelsis Deo*, has furnished the title to one of the great songs of the Christmas season. Appropriately it is called the "Angelic Hymn."

"Peace" is *eirene*, from which comes the name Irene. This was originally the name of the goddess of Peace. Thayer points out the various usages of this term in the New Testament. It first meant "a state of national tranquillity; exemption from the rage and havoc of war." Then it was used for "peace between individuals, i.e., harmony, discord." Next it meant "security, safety, prosperity." Fourthly, there was a special sense (used here), "the Messiah's peace." Fifthly, there is the distinct Christian conception: "the tranquil state of a soul assured of its salvation through Christ, and so fearing nothing from God and content with its earthly lot, of whatsoever sort that is."

III. DOCTRINAL VALUE. Peace is one of God's best gifts to man. It should always be recognized as a divine gift, not a human attainment. Christ's presence *is* peace.

IV. PRACTICAL AIM. To show the only way that peace can be found by individuals or by society.

V. HOMILETICAL FORM
   Theme: "God's Glory and Man's Good."
   Introduction: When the divine pronouncement of peace was made it did not come in a king's palace or at a conference table. The announcement was given to a group of humble shepherds in the open field. But the splendor of that historical moment far exceeded anything that man could have provided. For, "the angel of the Lord came upon them, and the glory of the Lord shone round about them" (v. 9). The Shekinah of God's presence overshadowed the shepherds as they heard the long awaited news that the Messiah had now come. Born that day in the city of David, He was to be a Savior, Christ the Lord.

   A. *Glory to God*
   In the familiar words of the Westminster Catechism, man's true aim is "to glorify God and enjoy Him forever." Some have found fault with this, maintaining that social responsibility should be given the priority over spiritual devotion. But what we must recognize is that it is only God's glory that brings man's highest good.

There are three ways that we may give glory to God. The first is by praising Him with our lips. This can be done by joining with others in congregational singing or by giving personal testimony to God's goodness and love to us. The second way is by lifting up Christ in our lives, displaying the implanted divine nature in true Christian living. The third way is by winning souls to the Kingdom. All of these bring glory to God as well as blessing to man.

B. *Peace on Earth*

One of the things that men desire most is peace. But they seek it the wrong way. The Bible throughout teaches clearly that righteousness must precede peace. We cannot have "peace with God" until we have been made right with God.

1. Political peace is what most men pray for. They cry out for the cessation of war. If we could only live in peace, everyone would be happy!

The only trouble with this is that it is not so. Times of national and international peace are not marked by moral progress, by love and joy in men's hearts. Often there is strife and hatred. Outward peace and prosperity have not satisfied man's deepest needs.

2. Social peace is desired by all good men. We deplore racial discrimination and the hate it engenders. We are opposed to any clash of classes. There must be freedom, with justice for all. But social problems are not settled by legislation alone. There must be the will to do right.

3. Spiritual peace is what man needs most. This can come only through the presence of the Prince of Peace. When He rules in our hearts, there is peace within. And that is where all true peace begins.

C. *Good Will toward Men*

The best Greek text reads: "among men of good will." And yet this is not quite an adequate translation. *Eudokia* can also mean "favor, good pleasure." Most scholars feel that this is the correct meaning here — "among men with whom he is pleased." That is, peace comes to those who are recipients of God's grace.

Actually, the two ideas are closely related. Men of good will are those who have submitted to God's will. The two words "good" and "God" are closely related. In fact, the former is derived from the latter. In the ultimate sense only the godly are good.

God can give His gracious bequest of peace only to those who accept His favor and so become men of His good pleasure. Jesus said not to the world but to His disciples: "Peace I leave with you, my peace I give unto you" (John 14:27). When we receive Christ into our hearts, His presence becomes our peace.

What our nation needs to do today is to cease its human search for peace and turn in repentance to the Prince of Peace. And it is the same path that individuals must take. Peace is to be found not in psychology or sociology but in Jesus Christ.

Luke 3

GOD'S FOURFOLD FORMULA

3:4. "Prepare ye the way of the Lord. . . ."
3:5. "Every valley shall be filled, And every mountain and hill shall be brought low, And the crooked shall be made straight, And the rough ways shall be made smooth;"
3:6. "And all flesh shall see the salvation of God."

I. HISTORICAL SETTING. Luke was the leading historian in the early church. His historical bent of mind shows up sharply in this chapter. The beginning of John the Baptist's ministry is dated as coming "in the fifteenth year of the reign of Tiberius Caesar" (v. 1). Tiberius was the second emperor of the Roman Empire. The dates of his reign are usually given as A.D. 14-37. But he became associated with Augustus in the ruling of the empire in A.D. 11 or 12. This would make the fifteenth year to be A.D. 26, which fits in well with the death of Jesus in A.D. 30 (perhaps six months for John's preaching and three and a half years for Jesus' public ministry).

Altogether Luke names five rulers and two priests in giving the historical setting for John's ministry. Pontius Pilate was governor of Judea (A.D. 26-36). Herod Antipas, son of Herod the Great, was "tetrarch of Galilee" (and Perea). His brother Philip ruled over some areas to the northeast of Galilee, and Lysanias over territory farther north near Damascus.

Annas and Caiaphas are mentioned as "being the high priests" (v. 2). The official high priest at this time was Caiaphas (A.D. 18-36). But his father-in-law Annas still exercised the authority. He had held the office A.D. 6-15, and then was succeeded by five of his sons, as well as his son-in-law. All were wicked men, more politicians than

19

priests. The nation of Israel was in desperate need of a spiritual revival. This was the burden of John the Baptist's ministry.

II. EXPOSITORY MEANING. John preached a "baptism of repentance for the remission of sins" (v. 3). That is, it was a repentance-baptism. He would not baptize anyone in water without requiring first a confession of sins (Mark 1: 4-5).

The Greek word for "repentance" means "a change of mind." Thayer represents well the thrust of this when he writes: "Especially the change of mind of those who have begun to abhor their errors and misdeeds, and have determined to enter upon a better course of life, so that it embraces both a recognition of sin and sorrow for it and hearty deeds."

III. DOCTRINAL VALUE. Repentance is often superficially thought of as being sorry. More adequate is the suggestion that it means "being sorry enough to quit." But the real sense is a radical change of attitude — toward God, sin, the world, and ourselves.

IV. PRACTICAL AIM. To show the need for repentance, and the results of repentance in bringing God's blessing.

V. HOMILETICAL FORM
    Theme: "God's Fourfold Formula."
    Introduction: "Prepare ye the way of the Lord." The picture is that of an Oriental prince making an official visit to one of his provinces. The people in those outlying districts busy themselves filling in valleys, cutting down hills, straightening out curves, and smoothing out rough places. They are eager for their sovereign to have a good road on which to travel.

So God was saying to Israel, and says to us today: "Prepare ye the way of the Lord." And then He spells out that preparation in four specific points, promising that if they obey, "all flesh shall see the salvation of God" (v. 6). This is God's fourfold formula for a revival.

A. *Fill In the Valleys*

The first thing an engineer does in building a highway is to fill in the low spots. In our Christian experience these may be of two kinds.

1. Sags in Our Souls. These are due mainly to two things. The first is neglect of Bible reading. If a person were to go without eating at all for a week or two he would feel very weak. So it is spiritually. A person can no more keep strong spiritually without eating spiritual food than he can keep strong physically without eating physical food. We must feed our souls on the Word of God every day to maintain our spiritual health. The second thing that causes sags in our souls is neglect of prayer. We need to realize that prayer is the breath of our spiritual life. Paul says, "Pray without ceasing." Don't stop breathing!

2. Low Spots in Our Living. It is deadly to live on low levels. Too many people live in the malaria-infested swamps of unbelief and worldliness. This can prove fatal.

B. *Cut Down the Hills*

These may be hills of hindrance, such as pride, self-will, self-assertion and the like. They must be attacked with determination and resolutely leveled if we are going to prepare the way for the Lord to come. It is working on just such matters that often precipitates a revival.

Or they may be hills of difficulty. We think of restitution that seems hard to make. More frequently there are difficult adjustments in our daily lives — at home, at work, at school, at church. Adjusting to both unfavorable circumstances and unpleasant personalities can sometimes be difficult indeed. But adjust we must, if we are going to have the divine blessing.

C. *Straighten Out the Curves*

The most obvious application is to crooked conduct. This can be devastating to our own spiritual life and destructive of the church. People will not overlook any dishonest business dealings, or even what looks shady.

But there is a more penetrating application to the little deceptions that are easy to practice. There is nothing so deceiving as the temptation to deceive. We rationalize and then find ourselves in trouble.

D. *Smooth Out the Bumps*

These may be thought of first as bumps and humps in our personalities. We all have some. They hinder those around us and hurt both our fellowship with other Christians and our influence on outsiders.

A second way of looking at it would be that these represent holes in the road that come through the wear and tear of daily living. A lot of traffic goes over lives in these busy days. Soon we have "chuck holes" of impatience and irritability. These need to be taken care of promptly.

Luke 4

AN ANOINTED MINISTRY

4:18. "The Spirit of the Lord is upon me, Because he hath anointed me to preach the gospel to the poor; He hath sent me to heal the brokenhearted, To preach deliverance to the captives, And recovering of sight to the blind, To set at liberty them that are bruised."

I. HISTORICAL SETTING. Matthew (13:53-58) and Mark (6:1-6) both record a visit of Jesus to His home town of Nazareth. But they place it at a later point in his ministry. There has been considerable dispute as to whether the two visits are the same. If they are, Luke probably placed it first as "a dramatic frontispiece to Jesus' public ministry."

"As his custom was" (v. 16), Christ went into the synagogue on the Sabbath Day — thus setting us an example for regular church attendance. He "stood up" as an evidence that He would like to read the Scripture lesson. Since He was handed the scroll of the prophet Isaiah, it is obvious that the regularly prescribed portion from the Law (Pentateuch) had already been read. The synagogue services began with the repeating of the Shema (Deut. 6:4-9; 11:13-21; Num. 15:37-41), followed by a prayer, the reading of the lesson from the Law, and then a portion from the prophets. It is claimed that in Palestine the Pentateuch was read through in prescribed sections over a period of three years, whereas the reader of the prophets could choose his own selection. Jesus chose Isaiah 61:1 (with the first clause of v. 2).

II. EXPOSITORY MEANING. "Anointed" is the verb *chrio* from which comes *Christos*, the "Anointed One." Thus there is a significant connection in the Greek which is lost in English. "To preach the gospel to the poor" is only two words in

Greek — *evangelisasthai ptochois* (literally, "to evangelize poor people"). "Gospel" means "good news."

"To heal the brokenhearted" is not found here in the best Greek text (cf. recent translations). But it is in Isaiah 61:1, which is quoted here. So we have included it in the sermon outline. In the Septuagint of Isaiah 61:1 "the broken-hearted" is literally "those who have been crushed in their heart."

The second "preach" is a different word in the Greek from the first. This one is *keryxai*, from *keryx*, "herald." So it means to "herald" or "proclaim." "Captive" is basically a military term, "one taken in war." "Liberty" and "deliverance" are the same in Greek, *aphesis*, which means a "release," as from bondage or imprisonment. "Them that are bruised" is one word, *tethrausmenous* — literally, those who have been broken in pieces, shattered, broken down, and are still in that state.

III. DOCTRINAL VALUE. Salvation is pictured here as healing from the brokenhearted, deliverance from captivity, recovering of sight, and freedom from oppression. The point is that salvation is more than the forgiveness of sins, wonderful as that is. It is health and liberty.

IV. PRACTICAL AIM. To show what the real nature of salvation is and what it does for the one who receives it.

V. HOMILETICAL FORM
   Theme: "An Anointed Ministry."
   Introduction: Jesus was anointed with the Holy Spirit at His baptism (3:22). "Being full of the Holy Ghost," He was "led by the Spirit into the wilderness" (4:1). There for forty days He was tempted by the devil. Having overcome, "Jesus returned in the power of the Spirit into Galilee" (4:14). Now in His "home church" He makes the Messianic announcement: "The Spirit of the Lord is upon me, because he hath anointed me."
   This anointing of the Spirit was for a fivefold ministry: evangelizing the poor, healing the crushed in heart, releasing

the captives, giving sight to the blind, and freeing the oppressed.

A. *Good News for the Poor*

Too often the church has neglected the poor, while it has
cultivated the cultured and ministered to those with means.
But one of the glories of Christ's ministry was that He evangelized the poor. When John the Baptist sent emissaries to
inquire whether Jesus was really the Messiah, the Master
gave as the climactic, final proof: "the poor have the gospel
preached to them" (Matt. 11:5) — literally, "poor people are
being evangelized." If we would follow in Christ's footsteps,
we too must minister to the poor. They are often more
responsive than are the self-sufficient.

The gospel is surely good news for the poor. It tells them
that they can have an inheritance in Christ equally with the
cultured, the educated, and the wealthy. God pays no attention to these outward circumstances.

B. *Healing for the Brokenhearted*

Today many people are crushed in their hearts — and for
many reasons. With some it is an unreasonable husband or
an untrue wife. For others it is ungrateful children or un-
godly parents. It sometimes seems as if almost everybody
has a bit of heartache, if not heartbreak.

But Christ came to heal the hearts that have been hurt.
His very presence brings peace and comfort to those who
accept Him. He is the Great Physician, and the only one who
knows how to heal broken hearts.

Never was this healing ministry more needed than now.
An ounce of balm for people's emotional disturbances can
often do more than a pound of cure for their mental ill-
nesses. This is a day when the Christian ministry is confronted with its greatest challenge — but also its greatest
opportunity.

C. *Release for the Imprisoned*

The sinner is in captivity to Satan. He has been captured

in the warfare of life. He is a prisoner of the enemy, not free to live as he knows he ought to live.

But Christ came to deliver the captive, to set him free. This again is good news.

D. *Recovery for the Blind*

In the Bible the sinner is portrayed as being dead, sick, diseased, imprisoned, living in darkness. Salvation is deliverance from all of these.

Out of compassion for their sad lot Jesus healed many blind men. But this was also a symbol of the fact that He gives sight to the spiritual eyes blinded by sin.

E. *Freedom for the Oppressed*

Many lives today are broken to pieces, shattered by sin, broken down under the burdens of life. To such the Christian can come with a message of hope. The compassionate Christ was also broken by sin — not His but ours. But His seeming tragedy on the cross has become a triumph for all who will accept Him. All who are in Christ Jesus are set at liberty. The oppressed are free.

Luke 5

THE SECRET OF SUCCESSFUL FISHING

5:4. "Launch out into the deep, and let down your nets for a draught."

5:5. "Nevertheless at thy word I will let down the net."

5:10. "From henceforth thou shalt catch men."

I. HISTORICAL SETTING. Whether this incident is the same as the call of the four fishermen in Matthew 4:18-22 and Mark 1:16-21 is still a matter of open debate. The best of scholars are divided on the question. Matthew and Mark place the call at the very beginning of Jesus' Galilean ministry. In Luke, on the other hand, the incident recorded here has been preceded by several miracles (4:33-41), as well as by a tour of Galilee (4:44).

II. EXPOSITORY MEANING. Jesus stood one day on the shore of "the lake of Gennesaret." This is the only place where this name is used in the New Testament. Matthew and Mark regularly refer to it as "the sea of Galilee," or simply "the sea." To the men who lived on its shores — Mark reflects Peter's point of view — it seemed like a sea. But Luke accurately calls it a lake, for it was only about thirteen miles long and seven miles wide. The name Gennesaret was derived from a small plain (about three miles long by a mile and a half wide) on the northwestern shore of the lake.

"Ship" is more properly translated "boat." Actually it was a small fishing craft, perhaps twenty to forty feet in length, such as can still be seen on the Lake of Galilee. "Nets" refers to seines, dragged through the water to enclose a large number of fish. One can see them today being washed and hung up in the sun to dry. "Standing by the lake" (v. 2) is better translated "lying at the water's edge" (NEB).

27

III. DOCTRINAL VALUE. Obedience to God's will always brings blessing. When Peter obeyed he reaped a rich reward.

IV. PRACTICAL AIM. To show how we may become successful fishers of men. By following the example of Peter we may hope for similar results.

V. HOMILETICAL FORM

Theme: "The Secret of Successful Fishing."

Introduction: It all happened on the shore of the Lake of Galilee, near Capernaum. The vast crowd of people pressed forward on Jesus until He was in danger of being pushed into the water.

Pulled up at the water's edge, or possibly on the beach, were two fishing boats. Climbing into one of them, Jesus asked its owner, Peter, to push out a little way from the shore. Then He sat down, as was the custom for Jewish rabbis, and taught the people who were thronging the beach.

Having asked for the use of the boat as an improvised "pulpit," Christ paid Simon a handsome rental fee by presenting him with an immense catch of fish. Jesus will not be in debt to any man.

A. *Pushing Out.* "Launch out into the deep."

Superficiality is one of the main secrets of failure. Shallow water cannot contain big fish. For success in any area of life one must heed the admonition: "Launch out into the deep."

"Nothing ventured, nothing won" is a principle that has wide application. Even in the business world it is the man who "launches out" into the deep water who makes the big haul. While others are content to catch a few little minnows in their tiny pond, this man pushes far out into the lake — and comes back with a boatload of fish.

Such a man was Bernard Gimbel. His poor father owned a little corner grocery. Bernard kept pushing out into bigger territory. Finally he envisioned something far beyond. Against the strong protest of his father and brother, he decided to enter the deep and dangerous financial waters of

New York City. It looked like sheer folly. But it made him a multimillionaire.

The same principle holds in Christian work. A succession of pastors — and the church is still the same size after a dozen or twenty years. Suddenly something happens. The "hopeless" situation springs to life, spurts down to the road to phenomenal success in a matter of months. What made the difference? The new pastor pushed out into the deep water of an aggressive campaign for reaching the lost in his community. He soon had a great catch of fish. The same thing is happening in large evangelistic crusades.

Courageous action is one of the great secrets of success. Timid souls never win great victories. Nor do lazy, inactive "saints."

B. *Putting Down.* "Let down your nets for a draught."

It was not enough for Peter to push out into deep water. There were fish there, lots of them. But he had to let down his net in order to catch them.

Occasionally a pastor, Sunday School superintendent, or church board plans a big project. Enthusiasm is gendered, excitement runs rife. Something great is going to happen!

But big talk does not guarantee big results. The "follow through" is what really counts. Planned projects can end up as pitiful problems. If the fish out there in the community are going to be caught, the church is going to have to let down the net in an earnest, persistent crusade of visitation evangelism. Seldom can the sophisticated "fish" of modern suburbia be lured by tempting bait, no matter how dazzling. If they are going to be caught, one must go where they are.

C. *Pulling In.* "They inclosed a great multitude of fishes."

When the Master issued His command to launch out into the deep and let down the net, Peter protested: "We have worked hard all night and caught nothing." It was foolish to waste any more time trying to do the impossible.

But fortunately Peter did not stop there. He went on to say: "Nevertheless at thy word I will let down the net."

When we are willing to realize that Christ knows better than we do, and follow His orders though they may seem foolish to us, we can hope to have success. Obedience is the most important secret of successful fishing for men.

When Peter obeyed, results came — surprising, spectacular. The net let down was filled with a large school of fish, so that it was beginning to break. Peter and Andrew waved frantically to their partners, James and John. Together the four men managed to haul in the net. The immense catch filled both boats until they were almost overweighted. Peter's obedience made it possible for his partners to share in the blessings he received.

Then Jesus said to Peter: "From henceforth thou shalt catch men." This was to be his supreme calling in life. And it is ours today.

Luke 6

MAKING MOUNTAINS OUT OF MOLEHILLS

6:2. "Why do ye that which is not lawful to do on the sabbath days?"

6:5. "The Son of man is Lord also of the sabbath."

6:9. "Is it lawful on the sabbath days to do good, or to do evil? to save life, or to destroy it?"

I. HISTORICAL SETTING. The two incidents from which our triple text is taken came at the end of a series of five conflicts between the Pharisees and Jesus. The first was over His authority to forgive sins (5:21). The second was a criticism of His associating with publicans and sinners (5:30). The third had to do with the question of fasting (5:33).

The first objection was due to a failure to recognize His deity. Only God has a right to forgive sins! Granted. But Jesus was God. So He had authority to pronounce men's sins forgiven.

The second was due to a failure to understand His humanity. Christ came to be one of us. He not only took upon himself a physical body but He entered into human living in a meaningful way. He became involved! The Pharisees were "separatists" — that is what the name means. Jesus got next to sinners in order to save them.

The third criticism reflected the overemphasis on asceticism on the part of the Pharisees of that day. The Mosaic law prescribed one annual day of fasting. But now the pious Pharisees were fasting twice a week (18:12). Jesus believed in living a normal, happy life that radiated joy instead of producing gloom. This was one great difference between Pharisaism and Christianity.

II. EXPOSITORY MEANING. The first incident in the Scripture lesson took place on "the second sabbath after the

31

first" (v. 1) literally, "a second-first (*deuteroproto*) sabbath."
The term is found nowhere else and its exact meaning is
unknown. It should be noted that the oldest Greek manuscripts have simply "on a sabbath."

"Corn fields" should be "grainfields" and "ears of corn"
should be "heads of grain." Actually the grain was either
barley or wheat, probably the latter. But in the British Isles
wheat is still spoken of as corn (cf. NEB). What is called
"corn" in the United States was unknown in the Old World.
Indian maize was given that name by the early colonists
from England simply because they were in the habit of
referring to all grain as "corn."

"Showbread" (v. 4) is literally "loaves of the presentation";
that is, "bread of the Presence." It was a beautiful type of
Christ as the Bread of Life on which we are to feed our souls.

"Watched" (v. 7) is a strong compound in the Greek, meaning "watched closely" or "observed narrowly." The Pharisees
were eyeing Jesus narrowly, hoping He would do something
they could criticize. This picayunish attitude caused them
to make mountains out of molehills.

III. DOCTRINAL VALUE. Sabbath observance is a part
of Christianity, as it was of Judaism. What we need to do is
to find out what Jesus had to say on this important subject.

IV. PRACTICAL AIM. To discover how our Lord would
have us to observe His day — what is in Revelation 1:10 called
"the Lord's day."

V. HOMILETICAL FORM

Theme: "Making Mountains out of Molehills."

Introduction: Little people major on minors. Big people
are busily engaged in things that really matter. This difference reveals the measure of our character. Are we majoring
on the truly important things of life?

The Pharisees were overly concerned about the minutiae
of Sabbath observance. In the Talmud no less than twenty-
four chapters are devoted to the subject. They found two

opportunities at this time to criticize Jesus and His disciples for failing to keep the man-made regulations of rabbinical Judaism.

A. *What Is Lawful?* "Why do ye that which is not lawful to do on the sabbath days?"

Jesus and His twelve apostles were walking through some fields of ripened grain. Hungry, the disciples began to pluck heads of wheat. They rubbed them in their hands, blew the husks away, and ate the raw kernels — one of nature's most nutritious foods.

All this was perfectly proper. The Mosaic law expressly said: "When thou comest into the standing corn of thy neighbor, then thou mayest pluck the ears with thine hand" (Deut. 23:25).

But the trouble was that this was on the sabbath day. The disciples were working. When they plucked the heads of wheat they were *harvesting*. When they rubbed off the husks in their hands they were *threshing*. When they blew the chaff away from the kernels they were *winnowing*. They really were breaking the Law!

These Pharisaic critics were typical legalists, making mountains out of molehills. As far as they were concerned the few innocent gestures of the disciples were just as bad as though they were working hard in the fields all day long on the Sabbath, harvesting, threshing, and winnowing their grain. The failure to make a proper assessment of moral values is the mark of a legalist.

B. *Who Is Lord?* "The Son of man is Lord also of the sabbath."

Over against all this rabbinical casuistry Jesus set His authority as Lord of the Sabbath. He had a right to declare what was allowable and what was forbidden. If He said it was all right for His disciples to eat some grain as they walked along, happily conversing with Him, then it was right.

Christianity is a religion of love, joy, and peace. These three virtues should characterize the life of every follower of Christ. These are the real mountains of religious experience. But the legalist turns these mountains into molehills with his harsh, unloving, joyless attitude. Everything is grim duty. Enjoyment of what one is doing is a sign that it must be sinful. Not so with Jesus. He lived life to the full and gave it new meaning and sacredness.

C. *Why Is Life?* "Is it lawful on the sabbath days to do good, or to do evil? to save life, or to destroy it?"

Why was the Sabbath instituted? Not just to make another regulation. Not to save religion, but to save life.

With Jesus life was all-important. He declared: "The sabbath was made for man, and not man for the sabbath" (Mark 2:27). The reason God ordained one day of rest and worship was that He knew man needed it — rest for his body, worship for his spirit.

What is proper to do on the Sabbath Day? This question has caused a lot of discussion. But Jesus had a very simple answer. Here it is put in the form of a rhetorical question: "Is it lawful . . . to do good, or to do evil?" The answer is obvious. Jesus himself put it in a categorical statement: "Wherefore it is lawful to do well on the sabbath days" (Matt. 12:12). Whatever is good for us and others — in the highest sense of "good" — is proper on the Lord's day.

Luke 7

THE COMPASSIONATE CHRIST

7:13. "And when the Lord saw her, he had compassion on her, and said unto her, Weep not."

I. HISTORICAL SETTING. The previous incident in this chapter is that of the healing of the centurion's servant at Capernaum. This officer sent elders of the Jews to ask Jesus to come and heal the servant who was at the point of death. The emissaries informed Christ that the centurion had built them a synagogue. He had helped others; now he needed help.

As Jesus approached the home, the centurion sent a further message. He was not worthy of having the Master come into his home. In fact, he had not felt worthy to speak to Christ directly. But all the Master had to do was speak the word, even at a distance, and his servant would be healed. The man thus exhibited a faith that made Jesus marvel. And his faith was rewarded.

From Capernaum Christ and his disciples walked down the western side of the Lake of Galilee to the village of Nain — a good day's walk of about twenty-five miles. Nain was situated on the slope of "Little Hermon," between Mount Gilboa and Mount Tabor in the Plain of Esdraelon (which separates Galilee from Samaria).

II. EXPOSITORY MEANING. For "bier" (v. 14) the margin of the King James Version has "coffin." But it seems evident that "bier" is the more correct translation, and it is followed in recent versions. At least it was not a closed coffin, for the young man "sat up" (v. 15). Probably it was just a flat platform of wooden boards on which the body was placed, as in Muslim funerals today. Burials in those days were crude and simple.

The young man had been dead for only a few hours. Because of the hot climate of Palestine and the lack of modern embalming techniques, it was required that the body should be buried the same day a person died.

III. DOCTRINAL VALUE. Luke portrays Jesus as the Son of Man. This incident is one of the many where he paints an unforgettable picture of the compassionate Christ. The Master has a tender love for sorrowing, suffering humanity.

IV. PRACTICAL AIM. To show how Christ comes to us in the emergencies of life to meet our needs fully. No situation is too hard for Him. No circumstances are impossible. No case is hopeless. "Jesus Christ is the same yesterday, and today, and forever." He can minister to us in our deepest sorrows and keenest sufferings, even as He did to this widow.

V. HOMILETICAL FORM

Theme: "The Compassionate Christ."

Introduction: Of Jesus in His earthly ministry it was said, "He went about doing good." He is still going about doing good. He is present at funerals as well as weddings. He shares our tears as well as our sunshine. Always He is there to meet our need.

A. *Compassing the Circumstances.* "A dead man . . . the only son of his mother, and she was a widow."

Nain was located on a hillside, right near the modern Arab village of Nein in Israel. Followed by a crowd, Jesus was walking toward the town. As He came past the cemetery and neared the gate of the city, He saw a scene that gripped Him with compassion. Men were carrying a bier, on which was lying the corpse of a young man. Behind the bier walked a lonely figure, a woman bent low with grief. No husband at her side, no son was there to attend to her needs. It was obvious that she was a widow and that the dead body was that of her only son.

All this Jesus took in at a glance. And He knew what that meant. Not only was the woman utterly bereft of loved ones;

she was completely uncared for economically. For when the husband in a home died, the oldest son became the head of the house — not the mother. He was fully obligated to provide for her. In this case, since there was no younger son, he was her sole support, socially and economically.

In those days a woman could not take a job as now — in office, store, or factory. This widow had lost her only source of income. To the sorrow of having lost both husband and only son was added fear of financial destitution. Her plight was indeed a sad one. The people of the city tried to show their concern. But her heart was utterly lonely.

B. *Comforting the Comfortless.* "Weep not."

When Jesus' understanding compassed the whole circumstance of the woman's tragedy, He was moved with compassion. He stepped to her side and said gently, "Don't weep any more."

She must have looked startled. If anybody had a right to weep, she did. Possibly she resented this intrusion. What business did He have interfering in her sorrow? To tell her to stop weeping seemed utterly heartless. This was the only release she had for her pent up grief.

But Jesus is never heartless, never unkind. He knew what He was going to do. Soon her weeping would be turned to rejoicing.

It takes confidence in Christ to obey His commands. But that is where faith comes in. If we believe that He knows best and that He is both able and willing to do that best, then faith becomes obedience.

C. *Commanding the Corpse.* "I say unto thee, Arise."

If telling the woman to stop weeping seemed unreasonable, ordering her dead son to arise sounded utterly ridiculous. But no sooner had Jesus said the word than the young man sat up. To prove that he was fully alive he began to talk. We do not know what he said. But presumably he spoke to his mother with tender love and thanked Jesus for restoring him to life.

The Master did not ask this man to follow Him in full time

service. Instead "he delivered him to his mother." The young man's first responsibility was in the home. His mother desperately needed him. Christ is concerned for all of life. He is interested in our social and economic, as well as spiritual, needs. And He is able to supply every need. He will do to trust.

Luke 8

LIFE'S THREE GREATEST THREATS

8:14. "And that which fell among thorns are they, which, when they have heard, go forth, and are choked with cares and riches and pleasures of this life, and bring no fruit to perfection."

I. HISTORICAL SETTING. Jesus was conducting a preaching tour of Galilee. We read that He "went throughout every city and village, preaching and showing the glad tidings of the kingdom of God" (v. 1). The two participles are literally "proclaiming and evangelizing."

Besides the twelve apostles, He was accompanied by "certain women" (v. 2). Three are named: Mary Magdalene, Joanna, and Susanna. Out of Mary Jesus had cast seven demons (not "devils"). Joanna was the wife of Chuza, a steward of Herod Antipas who ruled Galilee. Susanna is not further identified. These grateful women helped to provide food and clothing for the Lord; they "ministered unto him of their substance."

When a large crowd gathered on the shore of the Lake of Galilee, Jesus proceeded to give the people a parable. Recorded in all three Synoptic Gospels, the Parable of the Sower is one of the best known of Jesus' many parables. Fortunately, the Master himself gave a full explanation of its meaning.

II. EXPOSITORY MEANING. "Parable" comes from the Greek *parabole* — literally, "something thrown beside," and so a comparison. Unlike a fable, a parable is always true to life.

There were many footpaths leading through the fields. Hence in the process of scattering seed with wide sweeps of the hand as the sower strode across the ground, some

39

seed would fall on the hard-packed path. Here the birds would devour it. Also the soil of Palestine is full of rocks, so that some seed would certainly fall on shallow earth above a ledge of rock. Having no depth of root, the plants would soon wither and die. In both these cases there was no grain.

III. DOCTRINAL VALUE. This parable shows clearly that the results of gospel preaching depend not only on the divine sowing but also on the human response. Jesus was talking first about the varying reactions to His teaching. All four kinds of soil described here were to be found in His audiences.

But the same is true today. No matter how clearly and forcefully the Word of God is presented, the results are largely governed by the attitudes of the hearers. And in almost any large congregation all four types of soil will be found. Jesus did not win all his hearers, and neither shall we.

IV. PRACTICAL AIM. To show the importance of responding "in depth" to the preaching of God's Word. Hearers need to be challenged to realize that they, not the preacher, are responsible for what they do with the messages they listen to. If they treat the gospel indifferently or superficially, they are the losers.

V. HOMILETICAL FORM

Theme: "Life's Three Greatest Threats."

Introduction: The Parable of the Sower may more properly be called the Parable of the Soils. For the emphasis is on four kinds of soil on which seed is sown. No fruit results from sowing on hard or shallow soil. But in this message we wish to concentrate our attention on only one of the four — the thorn-infested ground. Jesus interpreted the thorns as suggesting three things in life:

A. *Anxieties*. The Greek noun comes from a verb which means "to be drawn in different directions." It refers therefore to the distractions of the mind, or to "the worries of life."

This is one of the greatest threats to spiritual growth. And it is increasing rather than decreasing today. The time was when life was relatively simple. A person could spend a rather quiet day at home, with no distractions.

But this is forever in the past. The doorbell, the telephone, the radio, the television — all these clamor for our attention. Life has become complicated, and so more divisive. One feels drawn in many directions at once, pulled to pieces. Most people today do not know how to be quiet and give time for growth.

Then, too, it seems that our worries have multiplied. High pressure advertising helps to bring this about. We purchase more than we should — "It's so easy to charge it!" — and then worry about our monthly payments. The pressure of this keeps us from taking care of the more important things of life. We are ashamed to pray for help in our folly. So we keep on worrying.

Anxiety is high on the list of causes of emotional disturbance and mental illness. But long before it gets to the stage where we have trouble with our social relationships, it may be cutting off our fellowship with God. Anxiety chokes faith; it strangles trust; it separates us from the Lord.

B. *Riches*. There never was a time when income was so high as it is for most Americans today. Our wages and salaries are larger, but not our savings.

But the very fact that we handle more money than ever before makes the threat of riches increasingly serious. There are so many ways to make "big money" these days. Why be content with a hundred dollars a week when one can make two hundred? But we are not content to stop there. We go on to three hundred, perhaps four hundred.

If we do not watch out, about this time money will be getting a strangle hold on our hearts. All we can think about is making more money. It is our meat and drink. With the thought of it we go to bed at night and get up in the morning.

The Psalmist warned: "If riches increase, set not your heart upon them." For most people today riches are increasing.

If we would save our souls, we must not set our hearts on riches.

C. *Pleasures.* Was there ever a time when the entire population seemed so pleasure-bent as today? Entertainment is big business — not only in hundreds of kinds of amusement centers, but right in our homes. Constructive conversation has been replaced by wasted time watching television. With too many people helpful reading has suffered the same fate.

The price paid for pleasure annually in the United States would make a staggering total, if we could add it up. But this can never be done. Presumably data could be collected, and a financial report given. But this would not represent the tragic total. For we have paid the price of wasted time, jaded nerves, dissipated emotions, and weakened wills. Pleasure presents herself as a beautiful maidservant, ready to wait on our every whim. But she ends up a monstrous slave master. Bishop Ryle comments: "The money, the pleasures, the daily business of the world, are so many traps to catch souls."

Luke 9

TESTS OF DISCIPLESHIP

9:58. "The Son of man hath not where to lay his head."
9:60. "Let the dead bury their dead: but go thou and preach the kingdom of God."
9:62. "No man, having put his hand to the plough, and looking back, is fit for the kingdom of God."

I. HISTORICAL SETTING. The major part of Jesus' public ministry seems to have been spent in Galilee. But now He was leaving there for the last time. Luke records: "And it came to pass, when the time was come that he should be received up, he stedfastly set his face to go to Jerusalem" (v. 51).

For the next nearly ten chapters (9:51—19:28) we have what is usually referred to as the Perean Ministry of Jesus. For the next few months it would seem that the Master spent most of His time in this territory east of the Jordan River. Perea is from the Greek *peran*, "across," and was the ancient name of Transjordan. It was ruled, along with Galilee, by Herod Antipas.

It would seem that Jesus first planned to take the shortest route to Jerusalem, straight south through Samaria. He sent messengers ahead to arrange lodgings for the night. But the Samaritan village where they inquired refused accommodations because the party was headed for Jerusalem. James and John, the "sons of thunder," wanted to call down fire out of heaven to destroy these wretches. But the Master rebuked their wrong spirit and led the way to another village (9:55-56).

II. EXPOSITORY MEANING. The Greek word for "lay" (v. 58) is from the same root as that for "couch" or "bed." So it means "to rest." Jesus had no place of His own where

He might rest His head. He who created all things never possessed any property, as far as the record goes.

"Preach" (v. 60) is neither of the common words translated this way, but *diangello*, which means "publish abroad, proclaim." It was time to proclaim the Kingdom.

In Christ's day one would literally "put his hand to the plough" (v. 62). One can still see occasionally a crude plow consisting only of a crooked stick being pulled through stony ground by a calf and/or a donkey hitched together. The single end is held by one hand.

III. DOCTRINAL VALUE. The cost of discipleship was a favorite topic with Jesus. It shows up rather prominently in all three Synoptic Gospels. Here three men are tested as to whether they really mean business. It is not enough to say, "I will follow." One must be prepared to pay the price of putting Christ first.

IV. PRACTICAL AIM. To discover what it really means to be a disciple of Jesus. This Scripture shows that it requires more than good intentions or initial enthusiasm.

V. HOMILETICAL FORM

Theme: "Tests of Discipleship."

Introduction: It costs something to be a disciple of Christ. In fact, it costs everything. The Master warned: "If any man will come after me, let him deny himself, and take up his cross daily, and follow me" (v. 23). Now He spells out the implication of this a bit more specifically to three individuals. In doing so He indicates three tests of discipleship.

A. *Complete Consecration.* "The Son of man hath not where to lay his head."

As Jesus and His disciples were going on their way to Jerusalem an eager aspirant confronted Him. "Lord, I will follow thee whithersoever thou goest," he cried. But the Master perhaps sensed here a superficial enthusiasm. Quietly but firmly He replied: "Foxes have holes, and birds of the air have nests; but the Son of man hath not where to lay his head."

Large crowds were following Jesus. In some ways He may have been one of the most popular men in Palestine. It would be great to walk near His side and bask in the brightness of His presence.

But there was another side which this man needed to know. Jesus had nothing in the way of material compensations to offer His followers. If they went with Him all the way it would entail deprivation and hardship.

Was this man willing to pay the price? We are not told. Perhaps like the rich young ruler, this man decided that the cost was too great, and turned away. That is what many still do today.

B. *Prompt Obedience.* "Let the dead bury their dead: but go thou and preach the kingdom of God."

On the surface these words seem harsh and out of character for Christ. From our Occidental point of view we are apt to picture a man whose father is lying in the coffin and Jesus will not even let him attend the funeral!

The facts, of course, are far different. In Oriental countries the oldest son carries full responsibility for seeing that his father is given a decent burial. It is very likely that this man's father might be expected to live for several more years. In the meantime, what about the need for the proclamation of the kingdom of God?

Discipleship demands prompt obedience. Soldiers answering the call of their country have to make sacrifices. They have to respond at once. So must the soldiers of the Lord.

C. *Firm Determination.* "No man, having put his hand to the plough, and looking back, is fit for the kingdom of God."

Following Jesus is "for keeps." It demands a crucial decision, backed up by firm determination.

On the surface the man's request seemed reasonable enough: "Let me first go bid them farewell, which are at home at my house." What was wrong with that? The problem was that an Oriental "farewell" might take anywhere from a few weeks to some months. Wedding feasts commonly lasted two or three weeks. It might take this man a year to settle all his family affairs and really leave to follow Jesus. By then it would be too late.

The man said: "I will follow, but. . . ." There must be no "buts" if we are going to follow Him. It must be: "I will follow — now . . . forever."

Jesus used the figure of a man starting out to plow a field. He becomes tired or distracted and quits before the job is done.

That is what has happened to would-be followers of Christ. Publicly they said, "I will follow Him." But the cost is so great they falter and fail. Jesus said that such would not be fit for the kingdom of God.

Luke 10

WHO IS MY NEIGHBOR?

10:29. "Who is my neighbor?"
10:37. "Go, and do thou likewise."

I. HISTORICAL SETTING. As Jesus came into the territory called Perea ("across" the Jordan) He realized that His time was short. The passover season was only a few weeks away, and He must be in Jerusalem at that time. What He did, He must do quickly.

So He "appointed other seventy also, and sent them two and two before his face into every city and place, whither he himself would come" (v. 1). Their task was to heal the sick and proclaim to their hearers the fact that the kingdom of God was now being presented to them. By repentance the people could enter that kingdom. They were also to prepare the way for their Master, so that His necessarily brief visits would be more fruitful.

After an interval — we are not told how long — "the seventy returned with joy, saying, Lord even the devils [demons] are subject unto us through thy name" (v. 17). Jesus made the significant reply: "In this rejoice not, that the spirits are subject unto you; but rather rejoice, because your names are written in heaven" (v. 20). Christ himself "rejoiced in spirit" that the Father had revealed heavenly truths to such simple folk as His disciples (vv. 21-24).

II. EXPOSITORY MEANING. The word for "tempted" is probably better translated "tested." Only when there is evil intent should it be rendered "tempt," and there is no direct indication here that this lawyer was trying to trap Jesus.

The term "lawyer" does not properly carry the same connotation that it has for us today. We think of one who argues cases in court. But in the New Testament it means an expert in the law of Moses, one who studied and taught the Law.

Among the Jews "neighbor" (v. 29) meant a fellow Jew. That is the point of the man's question. But Jesus rejected this concept emphatically. He showed that one's neighbor is anyone who is in need, regardless of race, color, or creed.

"Pence" (v. 35) is in the Greek *denaria*. The denarius was a Roman silver coin, worth approximately twenty cents. It was, however, the equivalent of a day's wages (Matt. 20: 2). Presumably the "two pence" would have taken care of the wounded man for several days.

Every "priest" (v. 31) was a Levite; that is, of the tribe of Levi. But not every "Levite" (v. 32) was a priest. The Levites who were not descendants of Aaron would act as assistants to the priests in the work of the Temple. A "Samaritan" (v. 33) was a half-breed, part Jew and part Gentile. The Samaritans lived in the central portion of Palestine, between Galilee and Judea, and were despised by Jews of both areas.

III. DOCTRINAL VALUE. There is an emphasis here on love as the basis of correct relationship both to God and to one's fellow man.

IV. PRACTICAL AIM. Jesus vividly underscored the truth that one should love everyone, without discrimination. Whoever needs your help is your neighbor.

V. HOMILETICAL FORM

Theme: "Who Is My Neighbor?"

Introduction: One day a lawyer challenged Jesus with the question: "What shall I do to inherit eternal life?" In reply Christ pointed the man to the Sacred Scriptures: what did the Law say? Correctly the lawyer quoted the very heart of Old Testament teaching, what the Master himself had declared to be the "first" and "second" commandments (Matt. 22:37-40). Putting together Deuteronomy 6:5 and Leviticus 19:18, the man said: "Thou shalt love the Lord thy God with all thy heart, and with all thy soul, and with all thy strength, and with all thy mind; and thy neighbor as thyself" (v. 27). Jesus told him to do this and he would have eternal life.

Eager to justify himself as having kept this dual commandment, the lawyer replied: "And who is my neighbor?" If Jesus said, "Pious Jews like yourself," the man would have considered himself secure. Even if the Master broadened it a bit to "your fellow Jew," the lawyer probably would have claimed that he met the demand.

But Christ had in mind a very different concept. To make the point vividly and unforgettably clear, He told what we commonly call the Parable of the Good Samaritan.

A. *The Robbed Traveler.* "Fell among thieves."

A certain man was going down the road from Jerusalem to Jericho. The Jericho Road was a winding mountain thoroughfare, descending steeply some three thousand feet in fifteen miles. As he walked around a sharp curve, suddenly some robbers sprang out from behind a rock. Disappointed to find no money on him — apparently he was walking, for no donkey is mentioned — they stripped off his clothes to take as loot and wreaked their vengeance on him by beating him half to death. Then they fled.

B. *The Religious Cleric.* "There came down a certain priest that way."

Thousands of priests lived at Jericho, where the climate was more balmy than at Jerusalem in the mountains. One of them was returning home after his tour of duty in the Temple. When he saw the bleeding body beside the road, "he passed by on the other side." He probably said to himself: "I offered this man's sacrifice the other day in the Temple. So I have discharged my responsibility to him." Perhaps the poor victim had put his last penny in the offering at Jerusalem!

C. *The Righteous Layman.* "Likewise a Levite."

As had the priest, the Levite kept as far away as he could from the robbed man. Perhaps a quick glance satisfied his conscience that the man was dead. If so he could not afford to risk becoming ceremonially unclean by touching a dead body. After all, there was no use in taking a chance! He wasn't to blame for the man's pathetic condition.

D. *The Renegade Samaritan.* "A certain Samaritan . . . came where he was."

This man was not an ordained minister, nor even a lay member of the congregation of Israel. He was a despised, rejected outcast. Apparently a man of some means, he may well have been a merchant on a business trip. Probably he had more reason to be in a hurry than either the priest or the Levite.

Yet when he saw the poor victim, he was immediately "gripped with compassion," as the aorist tense suggests. He did five things for the man: (1) "went to him"; (2) "bound up his wounds, pouring in oil and wine" — oil for balm, wine for antiseptic; (3) "set him on his own beast," walking beside the man and helping to hold him on; (4) "brought him to an inn," perhaps where the Good Samaritan Inn is situated today; (5) "took care of him," not only paying for the man's board and room, but promising to provide any more funds that might be needed.

Three basic philosophies of life are revealed in this story. That of the robbers was: "What's yours is mine, and I'll take it." That of the priest and the Levite was: "What's mine is mine, and I'll keep it." That of the Samaritan was "What's mine is yours, and I'll share it." Put a little more briefly and bluntly, these three philosophies might be summed up this way: (1) "Beat 'em up"; (2) "Pass 'em up"; (3) "Pick 'em up." Many in the world practice the first. Too often the church has been guilty of practicing the second. How many of us actually practice the third?

Having finished this fascinating story, Jesus asked who was neighbor to the robbed man. There was only one answer. Then the Master commanded: "Go, and do thou likewise." Those are His orders to us today.

Luke 11

PRAYER THAT PREVAILS

11:9. "Ask, and it shall be given you; Seek, and ye shall find; Knock, and it shall be opened unto you."

I. HISTORICAL SETTING. Luke's Gospel is the great Gospel of prayer. Six times Luke specifically mentions Jesus as praying where the other Synoptics omit it — at His baptism (3:21), after cleansing the leper (5:16), before calling the twelve apostles (6:12), before Peter's confession at Caesarea Philippi (9:18), at His transfiguration (9:29), and before giving the Lord's Prayer (11:1).

It was very fitting that when the disciples heard their Master praying, one of them should plead: "Lord, teach us to pray, as John also taught his disciples." Prayer is the very heart of the religious life.

In response to this request, Jesus taught His disciples the so-called Lord's Prayer (vv. 2-4). He followed this by the striking Parable of the Importunate Friend.

II. EXPOSITORY MEANING. Luke's form of the Lord's Prayer is somewhat shorter than that given in Matthew (6: 9-13). This is even more strikingly true in the earliest Greek manuscripts, which have simply:

> Father, let thy name be sanctified; let thy kingdom come;
> Our daily bread give to us each day;
> And forgive us our sins, for we also ourselves forgive everyone who is indebted to us;
> And do not lead us into temptation.

"Lend" (v. 5) means "grant the use of, as a friendly act." The "loaves" of Jesus' day were something quite different from our modern, sliced, baker's loaves of bread. They were like flat breakfast biscuits or small pancakes. The man wanted three loaves so that he could offer one to his guest, eat one with him for fellowship, and have an added one to offer his host for "seconds."

"In his journey" may be translated "out of his way." But in the hot season in Palestine people commonly traveled at night. So it was not necessarily unusual that a traveler should arrive at midnight. But it was inconvenient for the host. In those days it was the custom for the women to grind the barley or wheat each morning with little handmills, and make fresh "loaves" of bread for the day. Normally these would be eaten before night.

The Greek word for "importunity" (v. 8) is found only here in the New Testament. It literally means "shamelessness." When one knows his cause is just he has to be shameless in asking.

When "ask," "seek," and "knock" are listed one under the other, the initial letters form the acrostic ASK. However, this is true in English but not at all in the Greek. So probably the significance of this coincidence should not be stressed overmuch.

III. DOCTRINAL VALUE. The doctrine of prayer is of the highest practical value. Its importance in the life and teaching of Jesus is given a prominent place in Luke's Gospel. Here the emphasis is on prevailing prayer.

IV. PRACTICAL AIM. To discover the secret of answered prayer.

V. HOMILETICAL FORM

Theme: "Prayer That Prevails."

Introduction: One day the disciples heard Jesus praying — one of six such times recorded only by Luke. They were stimulated to ask Him to teach them to pray. They did not say, "Teach us how to pray," but "Teach us to pray." No matter what number of how-to-do-it books on prayer one may read, the only way anyone can learn to pray is by praying.

In response to their request, Jesus gave them the Lord's Prayer. It is marked by brevity and simplicity. Not a single word is wasted. The few brief petitions are right to the point. The primary petitions are for God's glory and kingdom. The secondary petitions are for our personal needs.

To encourage the disciples to pray persistently, the Master gave them the Parable of the Importunate Friend at Midnight. It consists of three parts and is followed by the application in the words of our text.

A. *Applying for Help*. "Send me three loaves."

Jesus portrayed a true-to-life situation — the hallmark of a parable. A man suddenly finds himself confronted with an embarrassing crisis. A friend arrives unannounced at midnight. Oriental hospitality requires that he be taken in for the night, but also that he be offered something to eat before retiring. Unfortunately, there is not a bite of food left in the house. To grind the grain and bake the tiny biscuit-like loaves at that hour is utterly impractical. What can he do?

There is only one thing: borrow from a friendly neighbor. So the man hurries to a nearby home and knocks at the door.

B. *Answering with Annoyance*. "Trouble me not."

Without getting up to open the door, the neighbor calls out: "Stop bothering me. My children are with me in bed." This would be literally true. In those days a "bed" usually consisted of a padded quilt stretched out on the floor. The entire family would lie down on this and pull a blanket over the group. If this man got up he would disturb the whole household. So he says, "I cannot rise and give thee."

C. *Asking with Persistence*. "Because of his importunity."

The distraught host was desperate. He had to have the loaves. So he could not take "No" for an answer. Shamelessly he kept on knocking and pleading.

Finally the neighbor rose and handed him the requested loaves. He did not do it because he felt friendly: he probably felt quite the opposite at the moment. But he decided he would have to comply sooner or later, and he wanted to get back to sleep.

D. *Application by Jesus.* "Ask . . . seek . . . knock."

If a selfish neighbor would answer a request because of the persistence of the asker, how much more will a loving heavenly Father respond to the prayers of His children. The contrast makes the lesson all the more forceful.

It would seem that "ask . . . seek . . . knock" suggest three stages of intensity in prayer. If one asks for something he feels he needs and that he has reason to believe is pleasing to the Lord, he may expect to receive it. If, however, the answer does not seem to be forthcoming, he should ask more earnestly. If the answer is still delayed, and he continues to feel that it is in divine order, he should get desperate and "knock." Sometimes God tries our patience and persistence. But He will finally answer. Prevailing prayer works!

Luke 12

THE RICH FOOL

12:20. "Thou fool, this night thy soul shall be required of thee."

I. HISTORICAL SETTING. Jesus apparently was still in Perea. Though some of the teaching here overlaps that found in Matthew's account of His Galilean ministry, it is probable that He repeated His main emphases in the new areas.

To "an innumerable multitude of people" Jesus said: "Beware ye of the leaven of the Pharisees, which is hypocrisy" (v. 1). He also warned: "Be not afraid of them that kill the body, and after that have no more that they can do. But I will forewarn you whom ye shall fear: Fear him, which after he hath killed hath power to cast into hell" (vv. 4-5). Most commentators feel this means that one should fear God rather than man.

The immediate background of the Parable of the Rich Fool was the request of a certain man: "Master, speak to my brother, that he divide the inheritance with me" (v. 13). Jesus protested that He was not appointed as judge over such matters. Then He issued the significant warning: "Take heed, and beware of covetousness: for a man's life consisteth not in the abundance of the things which he possesseth (v. 15). In other words, life is more than "things." The truth of the Master's statement is illustrated vividly in the parable that follows.

II. EXPOSITORY MEANING. In Christ's day a man's wealth was apt to be measured by the amount of land which he possessed. Here was a rich man with a large farm.

The Parable of the Rich Fool was apparently provoked by the covetous request of one whose father had recently died.

It would appear that he was the younger son. If so, he would receive a third of the family estate and his older brother two-thirds, according to the custom of that day. It looks as though this younger son wanted an equal division of the property.

The parable is followed by teaching similar to that found in the sixth chapter of Matthew, a part of the Sermon on the Mount. Right in line with the main lesson of the parable is this statement: "The life is more than meat [food], and the body is more than raiment" (v. 23). The climax is: "But rather seek ye the kingdom of God; and all these things shall be added unto you" (v. 31). Then Luke alone subjoins this beautiful saying of Jesus: "Fear not, little flock; for it is your Father's good pleasure to give you the kingdom" (v. 32).

III. DOCTRINAL VALUE. This parable emphasizes two important truths: the immortality of the soul and the certainty of the final judgment. The man planned to live a long time and enjoy his wealth. But God told him his time was up. He must give account of his life on earth, as every man must do.

IV. PRACTICAL AIM. To warn against the folly of a gross materialism that neglects the spiritual values of life.

V. HOMILETICAL FORM

Theme: "The Rich Fool."

Introduction: "The fool hath said in his heart, there is no God" (Ps. 14:1; 53:1). The man in this parable may not have been a theoretical atheist. In fact, he may have been in good standing in the synagogue. But he was a practical atheist. He lived his life as if there was no God to whom he was accountable. The fool is the one who says in his heart: "There is no God as far as I am concerned. I can live without God."

The man Jesus described was a fool for three reasons: (1) He thought more of his body than of his soul; (2) He thought more of himself than of others; (3) He thought more of time than of eternity.

A. *He Forgot His Soul.* "What shall I do?"

On the surface it appears that he was thinking of his soul, for he addresses it in verse 19. But what does he say? "Soul, thou hast much goods laid up for many years; take thine ease, eat, drink, and be merry." He seemed to think he could feed his soul on wheat and meat. No wonder God called him a fool!

The tragedy is that too many people today have not yet learned that material things do not satisfy the soul. If only they could have a better car, a boat, a beautiful home, expensive clothes, plenty of money to purchase entertainment — then they would be happy! But many are gaining all these, only to feel more miserable than ever before. A few years ago one man acknowledged that he was the wealthiest man in his state, but went on to say that he was the most miserable man in the state. Soon after that he committed suicide.

Material things cannot meet the spiritual hunger of the heart. The sooner people recognize this, the better off the world will be.

B. *He Forgot Others.* "I will pull down my barns, and build greater."

As is true in almost every Oriental country, this rich man was surrounded by multitudes of the poor. When he found himself burdened with a bumper crop, there was just one logical, humanitarian thing to do: distribute his surplus to the needy nearby. Instead he decided to build bigger barns in which to store his grain. But what good would this do for him? A man can eat only so much in a lifetime. What would happen to the surplus?

Greediness is one of the greatest robbers of mankind. It drives men on in an insane, insatiable quest for more — and more — and more. There is no end to it. Never satisfied with what they have. Always reaching out for something else. Covetousness robs a man of love, joy, and peace. It steals life's highest values and leaves him with only the bare husks of materialism. It robs him of rest and urges him ever on. Contentment — this he never enjoys. To think of others is to find oneself.

C. *He Forgot Eternity*. "Then whose shall those things be, which thou hast provided?"

When man lives only for this life he is living like an animal. Man was made for a larger world than this.

Yet most people give little thought to the next life. If you remind some people of the inevitable, inescapable fact of death, and ask what they will do then, they shrug their shoulders and say they are not worrying, or they will take a chance.

This attitude God calls foolish. And why not? This life lasts only a few decades, and then comes an endless eternity. There is no real comparison of their relative importance.

Suppose a man should have his choice between having on the one hand a life of unrestrained pleasure for a year followed by seventy years of tormenting misery, and on the other hand a year of hardship followed by seventy years of glorious happiness. If he should choose the first, would not everyone call him a fool?

Luke 13

THE FRUITLESS FIG TREE

13:7. "Behold, these three years I come seeking fruit on this fig tree, and find none."

I. HISTORICAL SETTING. Certain people reported to Jesus that Pilate had murdered some Galileans and mingled their blood "with their sacrifices" (v. 1). That is, they had been slain in the Temple while they were offering sacrifices there.

We have no secular confirmation of this event. But Josephus indicates that Pilate's administration in Judea was marked by many massacres. As has been said, "The Galilean zealots were notoriously turbulent, and Pilate was ruthlessly cruel." Probably the incident took place during some religious festival when the fires of nationalism were often fanned into flame.

Jesus himself mentioned another calamity that had recently transpired. At the pool of Siloam, in the southern part of Jerusalem, a tower had collapsed and killed eighteen persons. Again, we have no external testimony to this. But in those days it was not uncommon for walls to fall. In this instance it could have been due to either earth tremors or poor building — or both. Siloam is on sloping ground where a wall might easily not be too firm.

II. EXPOSITORY MEANING. The Galileans were thought by the Jews of Judea to be less pure and pious than they. The fact that some had been killed by Pilate showed they were even worse than the common run of the Galileans. So it was thought; but Jesus said, "No."

"Dresser" is literally "vine-worker," and so "vinedresser." "Cumbereth" is a strong term in Greek. It means "to make idle or inactive." Here the best translation is, "Why does it use up the ground?"

59

III. DOCTRINAL VALUE. It is easy for people to think that natural catastrophes are divine judgments. That they sometimes are seems to be indicated clearly in the Old Testament. At the same time, that they are not always so is proved by the Book of Job.

In the opening verses of this chapter it is evident that people thought the murdered Galileans must have been more wicked than other Galileans. Their tragic fate proved it. So also with the eighteen killed by the falling tower of Siloam. The Master denied this false concept. The righteous suffer along with the wicked in auto, train and plane accidents, as well as in such natural calamities as wind, fire, and flood. It simply is not true that tragedies are always punishments.

Jesus took advantage of this opportunity to give a much needed lesson on repentance. Instead of complimenting themselves on being so good that they had escaped disaster, the informers should realize that unless they repent they would all "likewise perish." The important thing is not to try to analyze the divine connection with physical calamities but to make sure that we are right with God.

IV. PRACTICAL AIM. To sound the warning that unfruitfulness can be sufficient cause for perishing. Are we bearing fruit as Christians. If not we shall finally be "cut down."

V. HOMILETICAL FORM

Theme: "The Fruitless Fig Tree."

Introduction: A horrible massacre had just happened. It was the talk of the town. Pilate had slain a group of Galileans right in the Temple as they were offering their sacrifices. Everybody was enraged — and scared.

About the same time a tower near the pool of Siloam had suddenly fallen and killed eighteen people. Certainly the victims of these two calamities must have been awful sinners.

But Jesus said, "No," — twice, emphatically. He warned: "Nay: but except ye repent, ye shall all likewise perish"

(vv. 3, 5). To enforce the point He told the Parable of the Fruitless Fig Tree. It was a sort of final warning to the Jewish nation.

A. *The Condition of the Tree.* "He came and sought fruit thereon, and found none."

A fig tree has one function: to bear fruit. If it fails in this it is useless.

This tree had been carefully cultivated. It had received all due attention. Yet when the owner came he found no fruit.

It was a picture of the Jewish nation, God's people. It had been planted in the Promised Land. Priests and prophets had ministered to its religious life. There was no excuse for its failure to bear fruit.

But it did lack the fruit of true piety. Too many of the religious leaders were hypocrites. They had the leaves of outward observance. But they lacked the fruit of inward character.

B. *The Condemnation of the Tree.* "Cut it down; why cumbereth it the ground?"

The owner complained to the gardener that he had been looking for fruit on this tree for the past three years, but so far had found none. There was no point in having the tree use up valuable space any longer. So he gave the order: "Cut it down."

It is difficult not to see a connection between the "three years" of the parable and the three years of Jesus' public ministry. For this length of time Christ had been confronting the nation with the command: "Repent; for the kingdom of heaven is at hand" (Matt. 4:17). But it had not repented. Instead it had rejected Him and His message. Now the three years were almost ended. Could there be any more respite?

C. *The Consideration for the Tree.* "Lord, let it alone this year."

The plea was made: give it a little more time. The gardener pleaded for one more chance for his fig tree. He wanted to cultivate and fertilize it once again. Perhaps it might yet bear fruit.

But to be fair he had to add: "And if it bear fruit, well; and if not, then after that thou shalt cut it down" (v. 9). Continued failure must ultimately bring judgment.

Jesus knew that the Jews would still reject him, remain fruitless, and so have to be cut down. A little later He cried out: "O Jerusalem, Jerusalem, which killest the prophets, and stonest them that are sent unto thee; how often would I have gathered thy children together, as a hen doth gather her brood under her wings, and ye would not! Behold, your house is left unto you desolate: and verily I say unto you, ye shall not see me, until the time come when ye shall say, Blessed is he that cometh in the name of the Lord" (vv. 34-35).

The cutting down could refer to the church of Jesus Christ taking the place of the Jewish nation as God's people. Or it could be related to the destruction of Jerusalem in A.D. 70. Perhaps both.

Are we bearing fruit? The term "fruit" suggests two things: (1) the fruit of the Spirit in Christian character; (2) the fruit of witnessing, in bringing other souls to Christ.

Luke 14

NO EXCUSES, PLEASE!

14:24. "None of those which were bidden shall taste of my supper."

I. HISTORICAL SETTING. In spite of the frequent clashes between the Pharisees and Jesus, He sometimes dined in their homes. One such occasion is described here. It was on the Sabbath Day, apparently the meal eaten after they came home from the synagogue. As usual, the Pharisees "watched him" (v. 1) with narrow, critical eyes.

"Before him" Jesus saw a man "which had the dropsy" (v. 2). It seems altogether possible that the man had been "planted" there to see what Christ would do — whether He would break the Sabbath by healing the afflicted man.

If so, the schemers were not disappointed. When the lawyers and Pharisees refused to answer His question, "Is it lawful to heal on the sabbath?" Jesus healed the victim and sent him on his way. Strict observers of the Sabbath would pull a donkey or an ox out of the ditch on the Sabbath Day. Why shouldn't He rescue this man?

The dinner became an occasion for a bit of practical teaching. When Christ observed some guests eagerly choosing the best places, He warned them of the folly of this. They were apt to be ousted in favor of some more honorable guest. The divine principle that works in life is: "For whosoever exalteth himself shall be abased; and he that humbleth himself shall be exalted" (v. 11).

Jesus also gave some advice to His host. Instead of inviting his friends, relatives, and rich neighbors, he should bring in the poor. They would not be able to recompense him, but he would have his reward in heaven.

II. EXPOSITORY MEANING. It is claimed that in the time of Christ the Jews ordinarily ate only two meals on week days, but three on the Sabbath. Strack and Billerbeck note: "The chief meal took place after the close of morning service — that is, more or less in the neighborhood of noon. The participation of guests in the Sabbath meal was a general custom."

Instead of "ass" (v. 5), the best Greek text has "son." The phrase would then read: "the son of which of you, or even only his ox."

III. DOCTRINAL VALUE. This Parable of the Great Supper teaches several truths. One is that every man is free to decide whether he will accept or reject the call of God. Not everyone who is called elects to accept. Those who are lost are not damned forever because of the arbitrary dictum of deity. They are lost because they refuse Christ's invitation, "Come." There is also here a strong emphasis on aggressive evangelism: "Go out . . . and bring in" (v. 21), even "Go out . . . and compel them to come in" (v. 23).

IV. PRACTICAL AIM. To show the importance of accepting the divine invitation rather than rejecting it, and to emphasize the responsibility which each one bears in deciding his destiny.

V. HOMILETICAL FORM

Theme: "No Excuses, Please!"

Introduction: One day Jesus found himself eating dinner in the home of a wealthy Pharisee. After healing a dropsied man, He turned His attention to the guests. He reproved the pride and selfishness of those who picked out the best places at the feast.

Then He spoke to His host. "Don't entertain just your friends, relatives, and rich neighbors. Invite the poor, the maimed, the lame, the blind. They will not be able to recompense you in this life, but you will get your reward in heaven."

When one of the guests observed, "Blessed is he that shall eat bread in the kingdom of God," Jesus used that remark as the springboard for a story. He proceeded to tell the Parable of the Great Supper. In it He dealt with invitations, excuses, and substitutes.

A. *Invitations*. "A certain man made a great supper."

1. "and bade many." The Orientals were fond of having big feasts. Servants were plentiful and so a man would be limited only by the cost of the food. Banquets were common, as they are apt to be today.

2. "Come, for all things are now ready." It was the custom not only to issue invitations ahead of time, as we do now, but also to send special messengers to notify the guests when the banquet was ready. Geldenhuys suggests the application here to God's feast for those who will enter the kingdom of God: "The first invitation refers to the promises of the Old Testament and the messenger who takes round the final invitations is especially Jesus "Himself." There is a further application to evangelism today.

B. *Excuses*. "And they all with one consent began to make excuse."

1. "I have bought a piece of ground." This man was more interested in viewing his newly acquired field than he was in enjoying the fellowship at the feast. He put materialistic interests above social and spiritual values.

This man is a type of those with whom "Business is first!" Nothing must be permitted to interfere with it. Other things are unimportant.

2. "I have bought five yoke of oxen." Here was a man who couldn't wait. Impatient, impulsive, he had to check out his new oxen. There was no time to be bothered with a feast.

3. "I have married a wife." This excuse has always seemed especially unreasonable. What better place to take his new bride than to a bountiful banquet? There they could enjoy a happy time together and meet friends new and old.

Unfortunately, most excuses are alibis. They are not backed up by reason but by personal desire.

C. *Substitutes*. "Then the master of the house being angry said to his servant. . . ."

1. "Go out quickly into the streets and lanes of the city, and bring in hither the poor, and the maimed, and the halt, and the blind." There is no enterprise in the world that calls for more urgency than evangelism. "Go out quickly" should ring in the ears of every Christian worker. While we tarry, millions more are born to live and die without knowing Christ as their Savior. The early church felt a sense of urgency which is too rare today.

The servant was commanded to go "into the streets and lanes of the city." That is where the people were. We must go outside our church walls and walk or drive the streets and roads if we are going to find those who need Christ.

The servant was also instructed: "Bring in hither the poor, the maimed, and the halt and the blind." Do we bring into our Sunday Schools and church services these kinds of people? Or do we pass them by? They are among those for whom Christ died.

2. "Go out into the highways and hedges, and compel them to come in, that my house may be filled." God is "not willing that any should perish, but that all should come to repentance" (II Peter 3:9). Godly people should feel the same way about the salvation of every last, least lost soul.

Evangelism demands not only a sense of urgency but a sense of compulsion. We must feel as Paul did when he wrote: "The love of Christ constraineth us" (II Cor. 5:14). These words found an echo in the motto of David Livingstone, carved on a stained glass window in the home of his birth in Blantyre, Scotland: "The love of Christ compels me."

Love for Christ and for the lost — this is the twofold motivation for effective evangelism. We must be willing to go out into the highways and byways of life in search of those for whom Jesus was willing to die. They must feel compelled by love — Christ's and our's.

Luke 15

THE SON WHO CAME HOME AGAIN

15:18. "I will arise and go to my father."
15:20. "And he arose, and came to his father."
15:24. "For this my son was dead, and is alive again; he was lost, and is found."

I. HISTORICAL SETTING. Two of the outstanding emphases of Luke's Gospel are lostness and salvation. The fifteenth chapter contains three parables of lost things: the Lost Sheep (vv. 3-7), the Lost Coin (vv. 8-10), and the Lost Son (vv. 11-32). The latter is more popularly known as the Parable of the Prodigal Son. The Parable of the Lost Sheep is found also in Matthew (18:12-14). The other two parables are found only in Luke.

Also Luke is the only one to record the story of Zacchaeus, the chief tax collector whom Christ won to himself at Jericho (19:1-9). At the close of that incident is found the key verse of this Gospel: "For the Son of man is come to seek and to save that which was lost" (19:10).

The opening two verses of Chapter 15 present a startling contrast. The first reads: "Then drew near unto him all the publicans and sinners to hear him." These despised renegades (collecting money for the Roman government) and "unclean" sinners were eagerly hearing and accepting Jesus' message. But the second verse says: "And the Pharisees and scribes murmured, saying, This man receiveth sinners and eateth with them."

It was evidently this attitude which caused the Master to tell the three parables following. The link with the first two verses shows up strikingly in verse 7: "I say unto you, that likewise joy shall be in heaven over one sinner that repenteth, more than over ninety and nine just persons, which

67

need no repentance" — or perhaps "think they need no repentance." The first part of this verse is repeated in verse 10.

II. EXPOSITORY MEANING. "Publicans" (v. 1) is more
correctly translated "tax collectors" or "tax-gatherers." The
publicani were wealthy Romans who received the right of
getting the taxes from certain large areas and turning in a
specified amount to the imperial government. They let out
the actual collection of taxes to local individuals, who were
underlings. These local tax collectors are the ones who are
mentioned in the Gospels. They were not publicans.

"Sinners" (vv. 1-2) does not necessarily mean wicked
men. The Pharisees applied this label to any who were careless about observing all the meticulous and multitudinous
regulations of "the tradition of the elders" concerning ceremonial cleanness. Actually it was almost impossible for the
common working man to keep all these rules. So he was
considered unclean, a "sinner."

"Receiveth" is a compound verb in the Greek meaning
"welcomes to himself." This is exactly what Jesus did, but it
cut squarely across the religious policy of the Pharisees.
"Scribes" were teachers of the Law. Most, if not all, of them
were Pharisees.

"With riotous living" (v. 13) is literally "living wastefully."
It was used in the sense of "living dissolutely or loosely."

III. DOCTRINAL VALUE. The supreme emphasis here is
on God's love for the lost, which leads Him to seek and
recover lost souls. Saving the unsaved — this is the main
theme of Luke's Gospel.

IV. PRACTICAL AIM. To see how salvation is intended to
reach every sinner.

V. HOMILETICAL FORM

Theme: "The Son Who Came Home Again."

Introduction: A familiar story in school readers is that of
the man who had the goose that laid the golden eggs. Greedy

to get all the gold at once, he killed the goose. Result: no more golden eggs.

This was the way it was with the younger son in our story. Not content with the daily golden eggs of kind parents and a good home, he wanted everything all at once. He got it, and then promptly lost it.

A. *The Possessor.* "And he divided unto them his living."

The younger son asked his father to give him his share of the family estate. According to the custom of that day this would be one-third, for the oldest son received a double portion — perhaps because he was obligated to care for his widowed mother.

Having received his part of the family fortune, the proud possessor started off down the road with his head high in the air. If he had seen the pigpen waiting for him he would not have been so eager and enthusiastic!

B. *The Prodigal.* "Took his journey into a far country, and there wasted his substance with riotous living."

The proud possessor had become a profligate prodigal. He evidently had not been used to having lots of money, with freedom to spend it as he pleased. Now he went literally "hog-wild" — and soon landed in a hog pen! "A fool and his money are soon parted." The prodigal quickly demonstrated the truth of this old proverb.

C. *The Pauper.* "And when he had spent all, there arose a mighty famine in that land; and he began to be in want."

Getting rich is ordinarily hard work and takes time. But getting poor is as easy as riding a toboggan down a slope; and usually one picks up speed and gets to the bottom very soon.

Thus it was with profligate prodigal. Before long he became a penniless pauper. And to add to his difficulties, a severe famine set in. Those with money found it hard enough to obtain food. For the pauper it was impossible.

Driven to desperation, the young man hired out to a farmer in that foreign country, who sent him into his field to feed the pigs. For a Jew this was bottomless abyss of disgrace. The pig was an unclean animal. The Jews were to keep away from hogs. But this young Israelite had gone so low that he actually envied the hogs because they had something to eat! Nobody would give him any food.

D. *The Penitent*. "And when he came to himself, he said . . . I will arise and go to my father."

Too often it is true that a person has to come to "the end of his rope" before he will come to himself and face reality. Sin is insanity. Now this sinner "came to himself," came back to his senses.

In striking contrast to the filthy pigpen and his own desolate condition, the pauper remembered the plentiful abundance at home. His father's hired servants were much better off than he. So he decided, "I'm going home."

But good resolutions are not enough. There must be action. Too many resolve to return home but never do it. This young man arose and went.

His father had been waiting for him. As soon as he saw the pitiful, emaciated figure in rags coming down the road, he rushed to meet him. There was first the kiss of forgiveness. The son's confession was cut short as the father commanded the servants to bring the best robe and put it on his son in place of the filthy rags. Next a ring was put on his hand. This was doubtless the family signet ring which authorized the son to transact business in his father's name. What amazing forgiveness! What full restoration!

This was not all. Shoes were put on his bare feet. The fatted calf was killed and a big celebration was soon in full swing. The prodigal had returned. The lost was found.

Luke 16

THE RICH MAN AND LAZARUS

16. "Son, remember."

I. HISTORICAL SETTING. Both this chapter and the
next begin with the statement that Jesus "said unto his disciples." It is clear that in the closing days of His ministry
the Master was spending most of His time instructing His
disciples in preparation for leaving them.

The same phrase occurs in both 16:1 and 16:19 — "a certain
rich man." But two different parables follow. In the first
instance it is that of the unjust steward. In the second it is
the story of the rich man and Lazarus.

The point of the Parable of the Unjust Steward (vv. 1-8)
is that "the children of this world (literally, "the sons of this
age") are in their generation wiser than the children of light."
That is, worldly business men use better judgment in pre-
paring for the future than do most Christians. Geldenhuys
puts it well: "In contrast with the diplomatic, clever conduct
of such people, those who are members of the kingdom of
light too often act unwisely and undiplomatically towards
others. Instead of behaving in such a manner that they bind
others to themselves, they act so that people are unnecessarily
repulsed."

Then follows the enigmatic command: "Make to yourselves
friends of the mammon of unrighteousness; that, when ye
fail, they may receive you into everlasting habitations" (v. 9).
Money is so often acquired and spent in an unjust way that
it is here called "the mammon of unrighteousness." But it can
be invested in kingdom enterprises. Geldenhuys asks: "Do
we use our worldly possessions in such a manner that there
will be persons in Eternity who will be glad to receive us?"

71

II. EXPOSITORY MEANING. It should be obvious that the language of the story of the Rich Man and Lazarus was intended to be taken figuratively, not literally. For "Abraham's bosom" (v. 22) cannot mean the breast of that man's body, which had been laid in a grave. Strack and Billerbeck write: "Lying or sitting in Abraham's bosom is . . . a pictorial expression to indicate the loving fellowship which exists in the beyond between Abraham and his pious descendants, derived from the love of a mother, who cherishes and protects her child in her lap."

"Hell" (v. 23) is not the Greek word Gehenna, but Hades. This word was first used as the name of the god of the underworld. Then it came to be used for the underworld itself, the place of departed spirits. It is the Greek equivalent of the Hebrew Sheol, which is translated Hades in the Septuagint. It appears that now all believers who die are immediately with Christ (II Cor. 5:8; Phil. 1:23), whereas unbelievers go to Hades. That Hades is not the place of eternal punishment is shown clearly by the statement that "Death and Hades were cast into the lake of fire. This is the second death" (Rev. 20:14). That is, the lake of fire is the final hell.

III. DOCTRINAL VALUE. The story of the Rich Man and Lazarus is a vivid warning of the horror of being lost. It also suggests that the wrongs of this life will be made right in the next.

IV. PRACTICAL AIM. To show the seriousness of life in this world as a preparation for eternity.

V. HOMILETICAL FORM

Theme: "The Rich Man and Lazarus."

Introduction: Any serious-minded person cannot avoid wondering about the seeming injustice of life in this world. The wicked prosper and live in luxury. The righteous are often poor and suffer hardship. It doesn't seem fair! How can we believe in a God of love and justice?

Our trouble is twofold. In the first place we measure things by material rather than spiritual values. In the second place, we measure things by time rather than eternity. The fact is that suffering is one of the important factors in producing the noblest Christian character. And perfect bliss throughout an endless eternity will more than compensate for all the lacks of this life.

To illustrate these truths vividly Jesus told the story of the Rich Man and Lazarus. It is a study in contrasts. The two men were at the opposite poles in life, in death, and after death.

A. *Two Men in Life*. "There was a certain rich man. . . . There was a certain beggar."

A greater contrast could hardly be imagined. The rich man "was clothed in purple and fine linen, and fared sumptuously every day." The beggar Lazarus "was laid at his gate, full of sores, and desiring to be fed with the crumbs which fell from the rich man's table: moreover the dogs came and licked his sores."

There is no direct statement that the rich man lived in immorality. But he was guilty of selfishness, and this is the very heart of sin. His dress and food were luxurious. He "fared sumptuously every day," oblivious to the harrowing hunger of the poor beggar at his gate. The least he could have done would have been to have a servant take some food to the sick, wasted form.

Instead all that Lazarus could do was to long for even "the crumbs that fell from the rich man's table." These would have fed him well. But probably they were swept up and thrown into the garbage containers. Only the dogs had pity on the poor man; they "came and licked his sores." They were more "human" than the rich man!

B. *Two Men in Death*. "The beggar died . . . the rich man also died."

The first thing that this verse says to us is that all men alike must die — the wealthy as well as the poor, the educated as well as the ignorant, the cultured as well as the crude. Death knows no partiality.

The second thing we note is the difference that took place at death. Lazarus may well have starved to death; the rich man may have eaten and drunk himself to death. Lazarus doubtless had no undertaker to care for his body, but his spirit was "carried by the angels into Abraham's bosom." On the other hand, the rich man "was buried." This does not tell us much. But we are fully justified in assuming that the funeral was a very elaborate affair, with a long procession to the place of burial. As far as the bodies were concerned, one was probably placed in the potter's field and the other given a burial marked by pomp and ceremony. But the story was different with their spirits.

C. *Two Men after Death.* "In hell . . . being in torments." "Abraham afar off, and Lazarus in his bosom."

An instant after death situations were suddenly reversed. The rich man, who had lounged luxuriously on thick cushions with a servant to fan him in hot weather, found himself "in torments." So severe was his agony that he cried: "Father Abraham, have mercy upon me, and send Lazarus, that he may dip the tip of his finger in water, and cool my tongue; for I am tormented in this flame." But there was no relief to be had.

In sharp contrast was the former beggar, now resting in Abraham's bosom. For him there would be no more hunger, pain, or suffering; "now he is comforted."

After death every man's destiny is fixed and irrevocable. Between the wicked and the righteous there is "a great gulf" which no one can cross. It is either Paradise or Torment; there is no place between.

Too late to receive any help himself, the rich man begged Abraham to send Lazarus back to his brothers, to warn them not to come to the place of torment. If one rose from the dead, they would listen to him. But Abraham sadly replied: "If they hear not Moses and the prophets, neither will they be persuaded, though one rose from the dead." This strong assertion receives striking confirmation in the case of another Lazarus who did rise from the dead. Instead of listening to him, the Jewish leaders tried to put him to death (John 12: 10).

Luke 17

REMEMBER LOT'S WIFE

17:26. "So shall it be also in the days of the Son of man."

I. HISTORICAL SETTING. Jesus was still giving private instruction to His own disciples (cf. vv. 1, 5, 22). He warned them against causing any weaker Christians to stumble (vv. 1-2). They were to forgive an erring brother, even seven times a day if necessary (vv. 3-4). He talked about faith (vv. 5-6) and service (vv. 7-10).

Verse 11 marks the beginning of the third and last part of Jesus' "Journeys on the Road to Jerusalem." "Through the midst of Samaria and Galilee" should rather be translated "between Samaria and Galilee."

As He entered a village in this area ten lepers met Him. They were required by law to stand "afar off." When they called to Jesus for mercy for their pitiful condition, He healed them. Only one, a Samaritan, returned to give thanks. The others were guilty of the gross sin of ingratitude. Once more Luke puts the Samaritans in a good light (cf. 10: 33-35).

II. EXPOSITORY MEANING. Jesus told the disciples that if they had "faith as a grain of mustard seed" they could say to a "sycamine tree, Be thou plucked up by the root," and it would obey (v. 6). The roots of a sycamine tree were considered to be unusually strong. The Jews had a saying that this tree could stand in the earth for six hundred years.

The fact that it is stated that the grateful leper was a Samaritan implies that the other nine, or at least some of them, were Jews. It may seem surprising that they mingled here, in view of the sharp animosity between the two races. But a common misery would tend to draw them together: they were all "unclean," outcasts from society. Furthermore

76

this was on the border between Samaria and Galilee (see above), where the two peoples were in close proximity.

III. DOCTRINAL VALUE. The doctrine of the Second Coming bulks large in the latter part of all three Synoptic Gospels. Luke's main teaching on it is in Chapter 21. But here he anticipates that with some foregleams of truth.

IV. PRACTICAL AIM. To emphasize the importance of being ready for the return of our Lord, not drawn away by the spirit of the world.

V. HOMILETICAL FORM

Theme: "Remember Lot's Wife."

Introduction: One day the Pharisees demanded of Jesus "when the kingdom of God should come" (v. 20). In reply He said: "The kingdom of God cometh not with observation"; that is, not by observing signs in the sky. Instead, "the kingdom of God is within you." In a sense it was already in their midst in the person of Christ, the King. It was also an inward, spiritual kingdom, not an outward, political one.

Then Jesus turned to His disciples. Said He: "The days will come when ye shall desire to see one of the days of the Son of man, and ye shall not see it." In other words, you will long for the coming of the Messiah; but you will have to wait. That is our situation right now, in the midst of hot wars and cold wars and strife between nations.

The Son of man would come suddenly, like lightning. But before that took place, He must suffer many things, even death, being rejected by that generation.

A. *The Days of Noah.* "And as it was in the days of Noe, so shall it also be in the days of the Son of man."

The days of Noah were times of extreme lawlessness. The record reads: "And God saw that the wickedness of man was great in the earth, and that every imagination of the thoughts of his heart was only evil continually" (Gen. 6:5). This condition is being too closely approximated in our day for anyone to feel easy about the outcome. When we pray for peace, for an end to the tragic waste of lives in war, we are reminded that our nation has wandered far from the paths of righteousness. Can we expect God to preserve and protect us when we flout His standards and desecrate His name?

The description of the people of that day seems innocent enough: "They did eat, they drank, they married wives, they were given in marriage." It sounds like "business as usual." There was nothing wrong with doing these things except that they left God out of their lives. But that made them god-less; and the godless shall perish, as these did in the Flood.

B. *The Days of Lot.* "Likewise also as it was in the days of Lot. . . ."

Here we are given a similar picture: they did eat, they drank, they bought, they sold, they planted, they builded." All of these things are innocent in themselves. But independence of God makes a man a sinner. And that is what these people were guilty of.

As in the case of Noah's contemporaries, we have evidence that the people of Lot's day were far from being morally blameless. For we read: "But the men of Sodom were wicked and sinners before the Lord exceedingly" (Gen. 13:13). Their particularly obnoxious vice has come down to us in the very term "sodomy." One of the most alarming things about society in the United States and Europe today is the shocking growth of this sex perversion. A recent essay in a leading news magazine revealed the fact that weddings are already being performed, uniting men with men and women with women. It was for sodomy that God "rained fire and brimstone from heaven, and destroyed them all." For the same sin, along with others, we face the danger of new fire and brimstone raining from the sky in the form of nuclear missiles. We can only pray for God's mercy on America.

C. *The Days of the Son of Man.* "Even thus shall it be in the day when the Son of man is revealed."

There are too many startling similarities between the days of Noah and of Lot on the one hand, and present days on the other, to leave us feeling very comfortable about the future. When we see the flood of filth pouring out of Hollywood, with its daring change of movie standards, together with the deluge of pornographic magazines cluttering our newstands, we pause and wonder. If ever there was a time when we needed a voice in our modern wilderness to call for repentance it is right now.

The closing warning is: "Remember Lot's wife." Her heart was still in Sodom, and she stood there looking longingly back at the city. She was left a pillar of salt, a monument of warning to those who are tempted to hold on to the world. One has to turn his back on the world in order to follow Christ.

Luke 18

THE MAN WHO PRAYED TO HIMSELF

18:11. "The Pharisee having taken his stand was praying these things to himself" (literal translation).

I. HISTORICAL SETTING. We have already noted that Jesus' main teachings on prayer are to be found in the eleventh and eighteenth chapters of Luke. In the earlier chapter we found the so-called Lord's Prayer and the Parable of the Importunate Friend. Here we have two parables together, that of the Importunate Widow (or unjust Judge) and that of the Pharisee and the Publican. In both cases the purpose of the parable was given. In connection with the first it is stated: "And he spoke a parable unto them to this end, that men ought always to pray, and not to faint" (v. 1). The second is introduced with these words: "And he spake this parable unto certain which trusted in themselves that they were righteous, and despised others" (v. 9). Discouragement and self-righteous conceit — these were the two things the Master warned against.

II. EXPOSITORY MEANING. "Faint" (v. 1) is better translated "lose heart." Two things are perhaps suggested. The one is that we should not become discouraged if we do not receive the answer to our prayers at once, but should keep on praying. The other is that the best way to avoid discouragement is to maintain an atmosphere of prayerful trust. This brings God consciously into focus against our daily problems and enables us to commit everything to Him continually.

"Feared" (v. 2) means to have reverence for. "Regarded" is better translated "respected." This judge had neither reverence for God nor respect for man. "Avenge me" means vindicate me" or "give me legal protection."

"Weary me" is a very weak rendering. The verb literally means "to strike under the eye" or "to give a black eye." This woman was getting desperate for help.

The Pharisees are mentioned some one hundred times in the New Testament. They were strict legalists who insisted on the meticulous observance of all religious regulations, not only those in the law of Moses but also those contained in the unwritten "tradition of the elders." They were the ones who taught in the local synagogues. "Pharisee" means "separatist." They were thus originally the Puritans of their day. By the time of Christ too many of them had become hypocritical in their religion. Jesus declared that some of them were clean on the outside but full of uncleanness in their hearts. They proved this in their jealous hatred of Him.

III. DOCTRINAL VALUE. Once more we have significant teaching on prayer. We are not only to pray persistently but humbly and sincerely.

IV. PRACTICAL AIM. To show the necessity of the right attitude in prayer. Above all, one must be utterly honest before God, for He reads our hearts as well as hears our words.

V. HOMILETICAL FORM.

Theme: "The Man Who Prayed to Himself."

Introduction: One of the most important lessons the disciples needed to learn was how to pray. They realized it and requested help. So Jesus taught them the Lord's Prayer — a perfect gem of brevity, simplicity, and straightforwardness. Its petitions are few but to the point.

To illustrate His teaching He told three parables. The principle of persistence was emphasized in the parables of the Importunate Friend at Midnight and the Importunate Widow. Humility and sincerity were the main points underscored in the Parable of the Pharisee and the Publican. It was told particularly for the benefit of "certain" (Pharisees) who "trusted in themselves that they were righteous, and despised others."

A. *Two Men.* "Two men went up into the temple to pray; the one a Pharisee, and the other a publican."

The Pharisees were the strict religionists of their day. They laid great stress on purity, but it was mainly a matter of maintaining ceremonial cleanness by avoiding contact with anything that would contaminate. They emphasized holiness, but it was of a formal, legalistic type. "Separation from sinners" — this was their motto. This tended to make them proud and haughty. The common people naturally resented this attitude. Self-righteousness is always offensive.

"Publican" is more accurately translated "tax collector." The men who belonged to this group were hated by almost all Jews. For one thing, they represented the foreign rule of the Roman Empire. Nationalism was strong among the Jews of Jesus' time. They eagerly awaited the day when they would be delivered from foreign oppression. For another thing, at least some of the tax collectors overcharged the people and this unpatriotic dishonesty naturally enraged the populace. Also the Pharisees considered that the tax collectors were rendered "unclean" by their contact with the Gentiles.

B. *Two Prayers.* "God, I thank thee, that I am not as other men." — "God be merciful to me a sinner."

The Pharisee "stood" — literally, "took his stand," probably in a prominent place where many could see and hear him. He was eager to put his piety on parade, to get praise of men.

He prayed "with himself." But the Greek says, "to himself." He was praying to himself, not to God.

One Sunday an exquisitely worded prayer was uttered in Trinity Church in Boston. The next morning an editorial in the newspaper observed that it was "the most beautiful prayer ever prayed to a Boston audience." The editor wrote better than he knew. It was prayed to the people rather than to God. Jesus taught His disciples to pray with simplicity and sincerity.

The Pharisee's prayer was a perfect example of how one should not pray. Instead of thanking God for gracious blessings from heaven, he thanked God for his own superior goodness. Actually all that he was doing was congratulating himself in public. To be thankful that we are better than everybody else shows the worst kind of spiritual pride.

But the Pharisee did not stop there. He proceeded to categorize "other men" as "extortioners, unjust, adulterers." Then flinging a contemptuous glance toward the nearby figure he added: "or even as this publican."

Then he proceeded to recite his virtues: "I fast twice in the week, I give tithes of all that I possess." This surely should give him high status in the eyes of God. What he forgot was that God was looking inside his heart rather than listening to his words. The attitude of pride and self-righteousness he had there, with contempt for his fellow men, was utterly godless. In the sight of heaven this man was a deep-dyed sinner.

In contrast the publican prayed a prayer that was a model of brevity, honesty, and humility: "God be merciful to me a sinner." That was all. But it was enough. He showed the genuine penitence of his heart by smiting his breast in consternation.

C. *Two Results.* "This man went down to his house justified rather than the other."

God can only justify those who repent and believe. The Pharisee did neither. The publican did both. His deep repentance demonstrated his true faith. For to obey is to believe.

The Pharisee justified himself, but Christ condemned him. On the other hand, the publican condemned himself, and Christ justified him. This is the way it works. Jesus concluded by saying: "For every one that exalteth himself shall be abased; and he that humbleth himself shall be exalted."

Luke 19

TEARS IN A TRIUMPHAL ENTRY

19:41. "And when he was come near, he beheld the city and wept over it."

I. HISTORICAL SETTING. Near Jericho Jesus had healed a blind beggar (18:35-43). While passing through the city, He saw Zacchaeus perched in a tree. This wealthy chief tax collector of the district was short of stature. Prevented by the crowd from seeing Christ, he had run ahead and gained his observation point.

The Master startled the little, big man by inviting himself to the tax collector's home. Overjoyed at this attitude — so different from what he usually received from the Jewish rabbis — Zacchaeus offered Jesus a hearty welcome.

But the people began to murmur and complain because Christ "was gone to be guest with a man that is a sinner" (v. 7). Zacchaeus acted quickly to squelch this criticism. Standing still, he said to Jesus: "Behold Lord, the half of my goods I give to the poor; and if I have taken anything from any man by false accusation, I restore him fourfold" (v. 8). The Master's reply settled it: "This day is salvation come to this house, forsomuch as he also is a son of Abraham" (v. 9). Zacchaeus was no longer "a sinner"! Then Jesus uttered the key verse of this Gospel: "For the Son of man is come to seek and to save that which was lost" (v. 10).

"Because he was nigh to Jerusalem, and because they thought that the kingdom of God should come immediately" (v. 11), Christ told the Parable of the Pounds (vv. 12-27). This suggested that the setting up of the kingdom would be delayed. Having spoken the parable, "he went before, ascending up to Jerusalem" (v. 28). It was His last journey to the Holy City.

II. EXPOSITORY MEANING. The exact location of Beth-phage is a matter of dispute. Both it and Bethany were doubtless situated on the slopes of the Mount of Olives. Bethany was evidently on the eastern side, where the "village of Lazarus" is today. But many scholars think that Bethphage may have been on the western slope of the mount, facing the city of Jerusalem across the narrow Kidron valley. If so, it was counted as being within the sacred area for purposes of eating the Passover. Putting all the Gospel accounts together, it seems evident that the colt on which Jesus rode came from Bethphage (cf. Matt. 21:1). "The descent of the mount of Olives" (v. 37) would be the west side of the hill, leading down into the Kidron valley.

Verses 43 and 44 seem clearly to refer to the destruction of Jerusalem by the Romans in A.D. 70, only forty years after Jesus uttered this prophecy. Josephus, the Jewish historian, agrees that there was not left "one stone upon another."

III. DOCTRINAL VALUE. Jesus was greeted as "the King that cometh in the name of the Lord." This was clearly a Messianic expression. In the minds of the people the man from Nazareth was more than just another prophet.

IV. PRACTICAL AIM. To show the need of real repen-tance, not just outward acceptance of Christ.

V. HOMILETICAL FORM

Theme: "Tears in a Triumphal Entry."

Introduction: It was the first Palm Sunday. As Jesus ap-proached the Mount of Olives He sent two of His disciples to secure a colt. He was about to ride into Jerusalem in fulfilment of Zechariah 9:9. In doing so He was presenting himself to the nation as its Messiah. But it rejected Him.

A. *The Cry of the Crowd.* "Blessed be the King that cometh in the name of the Lord: peace in heaven, and glory in the highest."

Somewhere about the top of the Mount of Olives, appar-ently, some people put their outer garments on the colt which had just been brought. Then they set Jesus on it. As the procession started down the western slope toward the city, many ran ahead and threw their loose outer garments on the path. As we would say today, they were rolling out the red carpet for Him.

It was a joyous occasion. We read that "the whole multitude of the disciples began to rejoice and praise God with a loud voice for all the mighty works that they had seen." These were the Galilean pilgrims to the feast of the Passover. They had seen the feeding of the five thousand on the shores of the Lake of Galilee. They had seen how Jesus made the blind to see, the deaf to hear, the dumb to speak, the lame to walk, the paralytic to carry his pallet. In their estimation He had given adequate proof that He was the Messiah.

So they greeted Him with a Messianic title: "Blessed be the King that cometh in the name of the Lord." These ardent nationalists from Galilee no doubt expected Christ to ride right into Jerusalem, overthrow the government of Rome, and set up His Messianic throne instead. This was the hour they had long waited for. No wonder they shouted for joy. As far as they were concerned this was the Messiah's inaugural parade.

B. *The Complaint of the Critics.* "Master, rebuke thy disciples."

In the crowd were some Pharisees. They became increasingly disturbed at the emotionalism of the multitude. They were also probably horrified that these pilgrims should acclaim Jesus as the King, the Coming One, the Messiah. To them this perhaps seemed blasphemous. In any case, for a shouting crowd to welcome a man as "King" was an extremely dangerous thing. The Roman rulers were apt to wreak revenge for this.

But Jesus answered: "I tell you that, if these should hold their peace, the stones would immediately cry out." So epochal was the occasion that if man did not respond all nature would burst forth into praise.

There are always those who will criticize any "religious

excitement." They want everything nice and quiet — and dead. The Book of Acts shows clearly that the early church was marked by excitement and enthusiasm. The movement of the Spirit is always accompanied by some movement of people's emotions. Every great revival has witnessed to this fact. The only alternative to life, expressed by some emotion, is death.

C. *The Cry of the Christ.* "He beheld the city, and wept over it."

The criticism of the Pharisees was but a foretaste of the condemnation of Jesus which would take place before the week was ended. No wonder He wept! He saw the doom that must inevitably result from rejecting the Messiah.

And so there broke forth from His heart almost a wail of woe. If only the people of Jerusalem had realized the significance of the hour. He was presenting himself as the fulfilment of Old Testament prophecy, as the Messiah of promise. This was Israel's greatest opportunity. But she turned it down.

What would be the consequence? The destruction of Jerusalem forty years later; the scattering of the Jews all over the world — a people without a country; persecution such as no other people have suffered, culminating in the horrible massacre of some five or six million Jews by Hitler. It was all "because thou knewest not the time of thy visitation."

Luke 20

RIGHTEOUS RETRIBUTION

20:16. "He shall come and destroy these husbandmen, and shall give the vineyard to others."

I. HISTORICAL SETTING. On Monday of Passion Week, as Mark 11 clearly indicates, Jesus cleansed the Temple (19:45-48). This appears to have precipitated violent opposition to Him on the part of the Sadducees. He had not only hurt their pocketbooks — for the priests operated the cattle market in the Court of the Gentiles — but had also challenged their authority. They could never forgive Him for this.

So they came to Him, along with the scribes and elders, and demanded of Him: "Tell us, by what authority doest thou these things? or who is he that gave thee this authority?" (v. 2). In return Jesus asked them a question: "The baptism of John, was it from heaven, or of men?" (v. 4). In other words, what was the source of John the Baptist's authority? This was a fair question, for the answer to it would be the same as the answer to their query. That is, Jesus was going to make His opponents answer their own question. This is always a wise thing to do.

The reasoning of the Jewish religious leaders described in verses 5 and 6 shows an utter lack of moral conscience. They were moved by considerations of expediency, not ethics. When they answered that they "could not tell whence it was" (v. 7), they were guilty of deliberate lying. It was not a case of "could not" but of "would not."

As a further answer to their question Jesus told the Parable of the Wicked Husbandmen (vv. 9-18). In it He clearly identified himself as the son sent by the owner of the vineyard, who symbolized God. Thus He clearly indicated His deity and the divine source of His authority.

II. EXPOSITORY MEANING. "Preached the gospel" (v. 1) is all one word in the Greek — *evangelizomenou*, "evangelized." "The chief priests . . . scribes . . . elders" were the three component parts of the Sanhedrin, the Supreme Court of the Jewish nation. They, not Jesus, were the ones who had authority to say what could be done in the Temple.

The "vineyard" (v. 9) represented the Jewish nation (cf. Isa. 5:1-7). The "husbandmen," or tenants, were the rulers of that nation (which in this case was the same as religious leaders). These leaders were given "a long time" to care for their responsibility.

"At the season" would be the time for ripe grapes, in August or September. The tenants were to pay their rent in kind, giving the owner his share of the grape harvest.

The three servants (vv. 10-12) represent the prophets of the Old Testament. "My beloved son" symbolized Christ. "Reverence" means "regard" or "respect."

The reasoning of the tenants has often been pointed out as utterly ridiculous. How could they hope to get legal possession of a property by killing the heir? But Geldenhuys has a good answer for this criticism. He says that "it is precisely Jesus' intention to call attention to the folly of the Jewish leaders' attitude towards Him by using as an example the foolish reasonings of the husbandmen."

Christ pointed out the consequences of the tenants' criminal action: "He shall come and destroy these husbandmen, and shall give the vineyard to others" (v. 16). That is, God will destroy the leaders of the Jews — and the people that identified themselves with them — and will give the vineyard (the true Israel, or people of God) to "others" (the leaders of the Christian church).

"The stone which the builders rejected" (v. 17) was, of course, Christ. Rejected by the leaders of the Jewish religion, He would become "the head of the corner" in the new church. The language of verse 18 was fulfilled partially in the destruction of Jerusalem (A.D. 70). Its complete fulfilment awaits the Second Coming.

III. DOCTRINAL VALUE. The doctrine of the Gentile church as the new people of God is highlighted here. Israel lost her special status.

IV. PRACTICAL AIM. To show the tragic results of rejecting Jesus Christ.

V. HOMILETICAL FORM

Theme: "Righteous Retribution."

Introduction: Every man must ultimately decide whether the authority of Christ is human or divine. If we realize that it is divine, we must submit to it. To fail to do so means that we perish forever. For He is the only one who can save us. To reject Jesus Christ is to sign our own death warrant.

A. *The Servants.* "He sent a servant. . . . another servant. . . . a third."

To show the seriousness of their rejection of Him as the Messiah, Jesus told the Jewish leaders the Parable of the Wicked Husbandmen. A man planted a vineyard and let it out to tenants, who were to pay him in kind. At the time of the grape harvest he sent a servant to procure the owner's share of the crop. But the tenants beat him and sent him away empty-handed. They did the same with a second servant, in addition to insulting him. The third one they wounded and cast out of the vineyard.

These three servants represent the prophets of the Old Testament. Many of them were treated shamefully, and some of them were even put to death.

B. *The Son.* "I will send my beloved son: it may be they will reverence him."

"Beloved son" in the Bible often means "only son." This was the owner's last resort. When the tenants saw him, they realized that he was the only heir. If they killed him, the family inheritance would be theirs.

This, of course, was foolish reasoning. But the point Jesus was making was that this was the way the Jewish leaders were treating Him. They thought that if they could get rid of

Him they could remain in control of the religious life of the nation and do as they pleased. They could cash in on their place of leadership to get wealthy while they left the people starved spiritually. Foolishly, they failed to realize that they were accountable to God, who knew their motives as well as their actions.

So the tenants cast the owner's son outside the vineyard and killed him. Likewise Jesus would soon be led outside the city of Jerusalem and put to death.

C. *The Substitution.* "He shall come and destroy these husbandmen, and shall give the vineyard to others."

The tenants had a good opportunity to enjoy peace and prosperity. They could have continued to care for the vineyard and would have been amply rewarded with their share of its fruit. But instead they were greedy. They wanted to keep everything for themselves. And in doing so they lost it all, plus their own lives.

This is the way it is for those who reject Jesus Christ and wish to hold on to themselves. They seek to save themselves and are lost forever. To find the best and highest in life one has to accept God's way and do His will.

Luke 21

SIGNS OF THE SECOND COMING

21:25. "And there shall be signs. . . ."
21:26. "Men's hearts failing them for fear."
*21:27. "And then shall they see the Son of man coming in
a cloud with power and great glory."*

I. HISTORICAL SETTING. The Olivet Discourse — so
called because it was given on the Mount of Olives — is the
only long discourse of Jesus given in all three Synoptic Gospels. It is also known as the Prophetic Discourse because of
its contents. It is found in Matthew 24 (and 25), Mark 13,
and Luke 21:8-36.

The occasion of the discourse is clearly indicated in verses
5-7. Some of the disciples called their Master's attention to
the beautiful stones and gifts that adorned the Temple. With
its marble walls nearly 150 feet high and its gold dome it was
one of the wonders of that day.

Then Christ made the startling prediction that the day
would come when there would not be left one stone upon
another. Distressed, the disciples asked: "But when shall
these things be? and what sign will there be when these
things shall come to pass?" The discourse is a response to
these two questions.

II. EXPOSITORY MEANING. It seems clear that Christ's
reply is divided into two main parts. Verses 8-24 deal with
the destruction of Jerusalem in A.D. 70. Verses 25-36 look
forward to the time of the end and the second coming of
Christ.

The signs that are given in the first section were all fulfilled in the first century. The frequent wars (vv. 9-10),

92

earthquakes and famines (v. 11), persecution by Jews and Gentiles (vv. 12-19) — all these are documented in the excellent commentary by Geldenhuys (Eerdmans, 1951).

The actual destruction of Jerusalem is dealt with in verses 20-24. "Compassed with armies" (v. 20) is literally "being compassed with armies." That is, when the siege began the Christians in Jerusalem were to "flee to the mountains." Eusebius records how they did this, making their escape to Pella, a town on the east side of the Jordan River and south of the Lake of Galilee. It was here that the Jewish Christian church was preserved after the horrible massacre that took place at Jerusalem in A.D. 70, when the siege ended in the fall of the city.

Jesus predicted this awful judgment: "And they shall fall by the edge of the sword, and shall be led away captive into all nations: and Jerusalem shall be trodden down of the Gentiles, until the times of the Gentiles be fulfilled" (v. 24). It is claimed that about 100,000 Jews perished when the city was taken, and another 100,000 were led away into captivity. Jerusalem has continued ever since to be "trodden down of the Gentiles." Though the Jews regained possession of a considerable part of Palestine, including the newer city of Jerusalem to the west of the walls, yet the Old City within the walls remained in Arab hands until 1967. The new state of Israel was set up in 1948. Just when "the times of the Gentiles" will end no one on earth can tell.

III. DOCTRINAL VALUE. The doctrine of the Second Coming, though often neglected today, bulks large in the New Testament. It is dominant in the only long discourse found in all three Synoptic Gospels. It is the main theme of what may well have been Paul's first two epistles (I and II Thessalonians). It also shows up prominently in II Peter, Jude, and Revelation.

IV. PRACTICAL AIM. To call attention to the signs of the Second Coming and urge all people to be prepared for it.

V. HOMILETICAL FORM

Theme: Signs of the Second Coming."

Introduction: It is popular today to scoff at those who believe in a second coming of Christ. What we need to remember is that His first coming was predicted for many centuries before it took place. But in spite of doubt and disbelief, He did finally come nearly two thousand years ago. Just as all the promises concerning His first advent were fulfilled at that time, so shall all concerning His second advent be fulfilled.

A. *Fearful Signs.* "There shall be signs . . . men's hearts failing them for fear."

We are not told what these signs will be. But in this age of space exploration we realize that a whole new dimension has been opened up to us. What relation this may have to the signs in the heavens we cannot tell.

Verse 26 certainly describes our times in a graphic way. Until recent years wars were confined to a small section of the earth. Then came two World Wars which forever changed the picture. But though fierce fighting took place on the continents of Africa, Asia, and Europe, it never touched the shores of North and South America.

We all know that this will not be true in a third World War. Intercontinental ballistic missiles suddenly raining death on our cities could well herald the beginning of that war. And every continent would probably soon be involved, especially with the wide spread of Communism.

But when things get their worst, "then shall they see the Son of man coming in a cloud with power and great glory." So "when these things begin to come to pass, then look up, and lift up your heads: for your redemption draweth nigh." This is the blessed hope of the Christian.

B. *Fig Tree Lesson.* "Behold the fig tree."

When the trees begin to put forth their leaves, we know that summer is near. "So likewise ye, when ye see these things come to pass, know ye that the kingdom of God is nigh at hand." That many of the things mentioned here are coming to pass in our day in a new and larger way, no well-informed person can deny.

What did Jesus mean when He said, "This generation shall not pass away, till all be fulfilled"? Some apply this to the destruction of Jerusalem in A.D. 70, only forty years later. Others take the Greek word for "generation" in another proper sense it has — "race." That is, the Jewish race will not perish before the return of Christ. It must be said that the preservation of the Jews through all their many persecutions, culminating with the massacre of 5,000,000 — 6,000,000 under Hitler, is nothing short of a miracle. But there is a third possible interpretation: the generation that sees the beginning of these signs will live to see the end. In view of the amazing speeding up of affairs in our day, we realize that ours could very well be that generation.

C. *Faithful Watching.* "Watch ye therefore, and pray always, that ye may be accounted worthy to escape all these things that shall come to pass, and to stand before the Son of man." This was the main concern of Christ. This was regularly His closing note of emphasis (cf. Matt. 24:42, 44; 25:13).

We cannot always interpret the signs of the times. We certainly are warned against setting dates. But we all must watch and be ready at any time for the coming of Christ.

Luke 22

THE LAST PASSOVER

22:15. "With desire I have desired to eat this passover with you before I suffer."

I. HISTORICAL SETTING. Passion Week began with the Triumphal Entry on Sunday. On Monday Jesus cursed the barren fig tree and cleansed the Temple. Tuesday morning He taught the disciples a lesson of faith as they looked at the withered fig tree. Perhaps on the same day we have the questions and answers given in Chapter 20. Either Tuesday or Wednesday was marked by the Olivet Discourse. Now on Thursday comes the Passover.

The chief priests and scribes were trying to kill Jesus, but they were afraid the people would mob them if they did (v. 2). Then, from their point of view, they had an unexpected stroke of fortune. One of Jesus' own twelve apostles, inspired by Satan, offered to betray his Master into the hands of the Jewish hierarchy. Overjoyed, they agreed with him on the amount they would pay. Did ever the love of money provoke a more heinous crime? Judas now sought an opportunity to betray Jesus "in the absence of the multitude" (v. 6). This dastardly deed must be done quietly and secretly.

II. EXPOSITORY MEANING. The chapter begins with the statement: "Now the feast of unleavened bread drew nigh, which is called the Passover." According to the Old Testament account (Lev. 23:5-6; Num. 28:16-17) the Passover was to be celebrated each year on the 14th Nisan, followed by seven days of the Feast of Unleavened Bread. But by now both names were applied to the whole period of eight days. The language of Luke here is almost exactly paralleled by the words of Josephus, a contemporary Jewish historian.

He writes: "This happened at the time when the feast of unleavened bread was celebrated, which we call the passover"
(Ant. xiv. 2.1).

The Jews used a lunar calendar: every month began with
the new moon. The Passover always came in the middle of
the month. That is why the date of Easter varies from
roughly the middle of March to the middle of April.

The Jewish leaders were afraid to arrest Jesus in public,
lest a riot ensue. The pilgrims from Galilee and Perea who
had acclaimed Him so ardently on Sunday could not be expected to stand by and watch their hero taken. So the rulers
sought to take Him "in the absence of the multitude" (v. 6).

"With desire I have desired" (v. 15) is a typical Hebraistic
construction, found frequently in the Bible. It means, "I
have earnestly desired." The Master was eager to have this
last fellowship meal, with its rich religious meaning, before
His death.

The "bread" (v. 19) was unleavened bread. The Jews
were very strict about searching their homes on the 14th
Nisan to make sure that there was no leaven (yeast) in the
house. "This is my body" obviously means "This represents
my body," for the physical body of Jesus was intact before
their eyes.

"Testament" should be "covenant." The Greek word is
diatheke, an agreement or contract made between two par-
ties. Our word "testament" (Latin, *testamentum*) means a
"will." But the Jews did not make wills, as the Greeks and
Romans did. Semitic peoples were strong on making cove-
nants. What we call the "New Testament" is really the New
Covenant which God had made with men through Christ.
All those who accept Christ as Savior and Lord enter into
that covenant.

III. DOCTRINAL VALUE. The Passover looked forward to
the sacrifice of the great Paschal Lamb for the sins of humanity. The Lord's Supper looks back to that central point
of all human history and memorializes it. Thus Holy Com-
munion is the Christian substitute for the Jewish Passover.

IV. PRACTICAL AIM. To show the significance of Jesus' inauguration of the Lord's Supper and what that sacramental meal should mean to us.

V. HOMILETICAL FORM

Theme: "The Last Passover."

Introduction: It was the last Passover which Jesus ever ate. True, it was not the last Passover of history, for both Jews and Samaritans still celebrate the Passover every spring. But it was the last Passover in a very significant sense. After Christ had died as the Paschal Lamb, the meaning of the old Passover had been fulfilled, and so the ceremony lost its value. This was the last Passover under the old covenant between God and Israel.

A. *The Passover Prepared.* "Go and prepare us the passover, that we may eat."

Finally came "the day," on which the Passover lamb was to be killed and cooked for eating that night. Jesus sent Peter and John into the city to prepare the meal. They were given cryptic directions. On entering the city they would see a man with a pitcher of water. This would be such an unusual sight — since women alone carried water jars on their heads — that they would have no difficulty picking him out. They were to follow him home. There they would find a large upper room furnished with rugs, cushions, couches, and tables. They would then prepare the Passover meal.

The rabbinical rule was that each lamb must be eaten between sunset and midnight by a group of not less than ten nor more than twenty. So Jesus and His twelve apostles fitted in very well with the requirements. Presumably the two disciples would purchase a lamb, have it slain by a priest in the Temple, and roast it for the evening meal. With it they would eat bitter herbs and unleavened bread, and drink "wine" — grape juice, whether fermented or unfermented.

B. *The Passover Repeated.* "And he took the cup, and gave thanks, and said, Take this, and divide it among yourselves."

Acting as head of the household, Jesus distributed the bread and wine for the meal. It is generally considered that this was the third cup of the Passover, handed round after the lamb was eaten. The fourth cup would then be the one used for the so-called Lord's Supper (v. 20). Christ was simply repeating the ceremony which had been observed by the Jews for over a thousand years.

C. *The Passover Replaced.* "This is my body. . . . This cup is the new testament in my blood."

The Last Supper became the Lord's Supper. For in these words we find Jesus giving new meaning to the bread and the wine. The bread symbolized His body "which is given for you." He added: "This do in remembrance of me."

So the Lord's Supper is a memorial meal, commemorating the death of Christ on the cross. But it also is a time of anticipation, for it looks forward to the return of our Lord (I Cor. 11:26). This gives it double significance.

Then Jesus distributed a common cup, that each one might drink from it in a closely knit fellowship. The fruit of the vine was red, symbolical of the blood of Christ "which is shed for you." Thus each time we partake of the sacrament we are reminded of the shed blood which atones for our sins and cleanses our hearts. Apart from the blood of Christ there is no salvation from sin.

Luke 23

THE INNOCENT MAN WHO WAS EXECUTED

23:4. "I find no fault in this man."
23:24. "And Pilate gave sentence that it should be as they required."

I. HISTORICAL SETTING. When Jesus was arrested in the garden He was taken to the house of the high priest (22:54). Here the Sanhedrin held an informal meeting, for it was illegal to hold a trial at night.

So in the morning it met in an official session (22:66-71). Two questions were asked of Jesus. The first was: "Art thou the Christ?" — that is, the Messiah. Instead of giving a direct answer, He said: "Hereafter ye shall see the Son of man sit on the right hand of the power of God." Obviously by "the Son of man" He meant himself. He would sit at God's right hand.

This caused the members of the Sanhedrin to ask the second question: "Art thou then the Son of God." He replied: "Ye say that I am." The Greek could equally well be translated: "Ye say, because I am." But probably Jesus purposely gave an ambiguous answer because of their wrong conceptions of the Messiah (Christ, Son of man, Son of God).

At any rate, the members of the Sanhedrin took it that He had answered in the affirmative. They condemned Him as worthy of death (cf. Mark 14:61-64). But the Roman government reserved to itself the power of capital punishment. So the Sanhedrin had to turn His case over to Pilate (23:1).

The charge on which the Jews condemned Jesus to death was blasphemy (Matt. 26:63-66). But they were smart enough to know that this religious accusation would carry no weight in a Roman court. So they trumped up a threefold political charge: "We found this fellow perverting the nation, and forbidding to give tribute to Caesar, saying that he himself is Christ a king" (23:2).

This, of course, was barefaced lying. Jesus had not been perverting the people. Instead He had affirmed positively that He did not come to destroy the Law but to fulfill it (Matt. 5:17). In the second place, all three Synoptics record that far from forbidding to pay taxes to Caesar He had emphatically said: "Render to Caesar the things that are Caesars" (Matt. 22:21; Mark 12:17; Luke 20:25). In the third place, He had carefully avoided claiming to be king — although the people had acclaimed Him as such in the so-called Triumphal Entry on the previous Sunday.

II. EXPOSITORY MEANING. The elders, chief priests, and scribes (22:66) were the three component parts of the Sanhedrin. They led Him into the "council" (Greek, *synedrion*); that is, they brought Him before an official meeting of the Sanhedrin. The Christ (22:67), Son of man (22:69), and "Son of God" (22:70) were all of them designations of the Messiah.

"This fellow" (v. 2) is a slurring expression of contempt. "Perverting the nation" was intended to convey the idea of causing sedition, which was the worst crime in Roman eyes.

"Thou sayest it" (v. 3) is probably purposely ambiguous (cf. 22:70). Jesus was a king, but not in the political sense that Pilate had in mind (cf. John 18:33-38).

"Fault" (v. 4) is hardly an adequate translation. The Greek word means "cause for punishment" or "crime." It was not the responsibility of a Roman court to decide whether a man was faultless. It was concerned with whether a man had broken the law and so deserved punishment for his crime.

III. DOCTRINAL VALUE. If Jesus had died as an actual criminal, obviously His death would have no value for us. But He was thrice declared to be innocent by a Roman governor.

IV. PRACTICAL AIM. To appreciate the fact that the innocent Christ died as a criminal in our place, for our sins.

V. HOMILETICAL FORM

Theme: "The Innocent Man Who Was Executed."

Introduction: Many innocent men have been put to death unjustly. But none compares with Christ. Not only did a Roman court three times declare Him guiltless, but His own conscience enabled Him to say what no other man could: "The Father hath not left me alone; for I do always those things that please him" (John 8:29).

A. *The First Declaration of Innocence.* "I find no fault in this man" (23:4).

The Jewish leaders had brought a threefold political charge against Jesus. They said that He was: (1) "perverting the nation"; (2) "forbidding to give tribute to Caesar"; (3) "saying that he himself is Christ a King." All of these were very serious accusations. In fact, any one of them alone would have been sufficient cause for executing Jesus as an enemy of the Roman Empire. Of course, the religious leaders were well aware of this.

Pilate talked with Christ. He evidently became satisfied that the charges were all false. For he came back to the chief priests and the people with the verdict: "I find no fault in this man." That is, "He is not guilty."

B. *The Second Declaration.* "I, having examined him before you, have found no fault in this man touching those things whereof ye accuse him" (23:14).

Not at all happy with Pilate's attitude, the religious leaders "were the more fierce, saying, He stirreth up the people" (v. 5). They were bound to prove Him a trouble-maker.

When they inadvertently mentioned Galilee, Pilate tried to get rid of the responsibility of deciding Jesus' case by sending Him to Herod Antipas, ruler of Galilee, who had come for the Passover. But this proved to be no escape. Herod mocked Christ and sent Him right back to Pilate.

Pilate then called together the Jewish rulers. He had examined Jesus in open court and had not found Him guilty of any charges laid against Him. Even Herod had found nothing wrong with Him. Pilate suggested that he have Jesus beaten and then release Him.

By this time the religious leaders were getting desperate. It looked as though they were going to lose their case. So they began yelling in unison: "Away with this man. . . . Crucify him, crucify him" (vv. 18, 21).

C. *The Third Declaration.* "I have found no cause of death in him" (23:22).

This should have settled it. If Pilate had been a man of honesty and moral courage he would have climaxed his three declarations of innocence with the verdict, "Not Guilty."

But the governor was weak and wobbly. As the pressures increased, he "caved in." In one of the greatest miscarriages of justice in all history, "Pilate gave sentence that it should be as they required" (v. 24). In doing so he abdicated all right to be a ruler and judge. He was a political puppet.

So he released to the people one who was a murderer and insurrectionist, and ordered the Prince of Life to be put to death. And that is virtually what people have been doing ever since.

Our hearts ought to be stirred with fresh gratitude that Jesus, the sinless One, was willing to die in our place. We should pledge Him our full love and loyalty.

Luke 24

THE UNCONSCIOUS PRESENCE

24:15. "Jesus himself drew near, and went with them."

I. HISTORICAL SETTING. The last chapter in the life of Christ is the story of the Resurrection. This is shown in each of the Gospels.

In common with Matthew, Luke tells of the visit of certain women to the sepulcher on Sunday morning. But he adds a note as to their purpose. They were "bringing the spices which they had prepared" (v. 1), in order to anoint the corpse of Christ.

Instead of finding the body they were confronted by two angels, who declared: "He is not here, but is risen" (v. 6). The women promptly reported the matter to "the eleven" — Judas was gone. The disciples reacted in typical masculine fashion: "And their words seemed to them as idle tales, and they believed them not" (v. 11). But Peter — with John (cf. John 20:2-10) — did go to the tomb to investigate. Sure enough, the body was gone. But, strangely, the grave clothes were lying there empty. It was all beyond Peter's comprehension.

II. EXPOSITORY MEANING. The location of Emmaus (v. 13) is still uncertain. "Threescore furlongs" (Greek, *stadious*) was about seven miles and a half. "Cleopas" (v. 18) is mentioned only here, and nothing further is known about him.

The Messianic concepts and expectations of the Jews are revealed strikingly in the words of these two disciples: "But we trusted that it had been he which should have redeemed Israel" (v. 21). That is, they believed that Jesus was the Messiah. So they expected Him to expel the Romans and "redeem" the nation of Israel from foreign domination. Doubtless they were among the ones who acclaimed him King in the Triumphal Entry just a week before this. But instead of His driving out the Romans, He had allowed them to put Him to death. When this happened, all Messianic hopes disappeared. What these disciples did not realize, of course, was that the very death of Jesus was to bring a larger redemption in spiritual salvation.

"Christ" (v. 26) should be translated "the Messiah." What Jesus proceeded to show these Jewish believers was that their "scriptures" (our Old Testament) taught that the Messiah was to suffer before He entered His glory. Christ started with Moses and went through the Old Testament, proving this point. He doubtless called attention especially to Psalm 22 and Isaiah 53. In verse 44 we have the threefold division of the Hebrew canon: "the law of Moses . . . the prophets . . . the psalms" (or Writings). Our thirty-nine books were classified under these three headings.

III. DOCTRINAL VALUE. The spiritual presence of Jesus with each of His own is a precious truth. If we believe that God is Spirit, we know that He can be with all of us all the time.

IV. PRACTICAL AIM. To emphasize the fact that Jesus walks life's road with us and that we ought to be more conscious of His presence.

V. HOMILETICAL FORM

Theme: "The Unconscious Presence."

Introduction: Jesus is "The Christ of Every Road." The pitiful thing is that too often we are unconscious of His presence. We need to have our spiritual eyes opened so that we can see Him. For He is there.

A. *Sad Hearts.* "What matter of communications are these that ye have one to another, as ye walk, and are sad?" (24:17).

Two disciples of Christ were walking home one Sunday afternoon from Jerusalem to Emmaus. Their hearts were heavy, their faces sad. They had believed that Jesus of Naza-reth was the Messiah. They had joined in the triumphal procession the Sunday before, as the Passover pilgrims shouted "Blessed be the King that cometh in the name of the Lord" (19:38). They had expected Him to ride into Jerusalem, drive out the Romans, and set up His Messianic kingdom.

But a week from that day everything was different. In almost stupefied unbelief they had heard Pilate give in to the pressure of the crowd and order Jesus crucified. They had followed Him outside the gate to the place of execution. There with agonized hearts they had heard His cries and seen Him expire. And with that all their Messianic hopes expired, too. No wonder they were sad.

All this they related to the stranger who had joined them on the road and now walked by their side. So clouded by sorrow was their vision that they did not recognize who He was.

B. *Slow Hearts.* "O fools, and slow of heart to believe all that the prophets have spoken" (24:25).

When they had finished their recital, Jesus chided them for their failure to understand their Scriptures. "And beginning at Moses and all the prophets, he expounded unto them in all the scriptures the things concerning himself" (v. 27).

Probably everyone who has read that statement carefully has thought: "How I would like to have been there and to have heard the Great Teacher expound the Christology of the Old Testament!" It would be a rare treat indeed. But Jesus promised to give us the Holy Spirit who would teach us all things (John 14:26). With His help we can understand the Scriptures.

C. *Seeing Hearts.* "And their eyes were opened, and they knew him" (24:31).

How long Jesus had been with them we are not told. But it was probably an hour or two. All that time they had not recognized Him.

As they approached their home, the Stranger naturally

acted as though He was going on His way. But since it was getting toward night, they constrained Him to stay with them.

It was at the supper table that it happened. In the old familiar way "he took bread, and blessed it, and brake, and gave to them" (v. 30). Suddenly they recognized who it was. But even as they really saw Him for the first time that day, He vanished out of their sight.

Then the meaning of that afternoon's conversation dawned upon them. With awed tones they exclaimed: "Did not our heart burn within us, while he talked with us by the way, and while he opened to us the scriptures?" Always our hearts burn when His voice speaks in our souls. What the world sorely needs is more burning hearts and less careless, cold, cruel hearts.

D. *Sharing Hearts.* "And they rose up the same hour, and returned to Jerusalem" (24:33).

They were weary. They had walked the seven miles from Jerusalem. It was late and would probably be dark before they reached the city.

But this news was too wonderful to keep to themselves. They must share it with the sorrowing disciples back in Jerusalem.

So, tired though they were, they headed right back to town. A bit footsore they finally arrived. When they reached the Upper Room they found the eleven gathered, with a few others.

Before the Emmaus disciples could get in a word, some of the Jerusalem folk excitedly said: "The Lord is risen indeed, and hath appeared to Simon" (v. 34). Poor Peter; he had been in misery since denying his Lord. Compassionately Christ met him that day and forgave him. Now there was a general rejoicing together.

What we need to do is to recognize the presence of Christ with us on every mile, even at every step, of life's way. He need not be for us "the Unconscious Presence."

BIBLIOGRAPHY

Arndt, William F., *The Gospel According to St. Luke*. "Bible Commentary." St Louis: Concordia Publishing House, 1956.

Barclay, William, *The Gospel of Luke*. "The Daily Study Bible." 2nd ed. Philadelphia: Westminster Press, 1956.

Bruce, A. B., *The Synoptic Gospels*. "The Expositor's Greek Testament." Edited by W. Robertson Nicoll. Grand Rapids: Wm. B. Eerdmans Publishing Co., n.d.

Burton, Henry, *The Gospel According to St. Luke*. "The Expositor's Bible." Edited by W. R. Nicoll. New York: A. C. Armstrong and Son, 1896.

Creed, J. M., *The Gospel According to St. Luke*. London: Macmillan and Co., 1930.

Erdman, Charles R., *The Gospel of Luke*. Philadelphia: Westminster Press, 1931.

Farrar, F. W., *The Gospel According to St. Luke*. "Cambridge Greek Testament." Cambridge: University Press, 1884.

Geldenhuys, Norval, *Commentary on the Gospel of Luke*. "New International Commentary on the New Testament." Grand Rapids: Wm. B. Eerdmans Publishing Co., 1951.

Godet, F. L., *Commentary on the Gospel of Luke*. Grand Rapids: Zondervan Publishing House, n.d.

Leany, A. R. C., *A Commentary on the Gospel According to St. Luke*. "Harper's New Testament Commentaries." New York: Harper & Brothers, 1958.

Lenski, R. C. H., *The Interpretation of St. Luke's Gospel*. Columbus, O.: Wartburg Press, 1946.

Maclaren, Alexander, *Expositions of Holy Scripture*. Vol. IX. Grand Rapids: Wm. B. Eerdmans Publishing Co., 1944 (reprint).

Manson, William, *The Gospel of Luke*. "The Moffatt New Testament Commentary." New York: Harper and Brothers, 1930.

Miller, Donald G., *The Gospel According to Luke*. "The Layman's Bible Commentary." Edited by Balmer H. Kelly. Richmond, Va.: John Knox Press, 1959.

Morgan, G. Campbell, *The Gospel According to Luke*. New York: Fleming H. Revell Co., 1931.

Plummer, Alfred, *A Critical and Exegetical Commentary on the Gospel According to St. Luke*. "The International Critical Commentary." New York: Charles Scribner's Sons, 1896.

Plumptre, E. H., *The Gospel According to St. Luke*. "Commentary on the Whole Bible." Edited by C. J. Ellicott. Grand Rapids: Zondervan Publishing House, 1954 (reprint).

Ragg, Lonsdale, *St. Luke*. "Westminster Commentaries." London: Methuen & Co., 1922.

Date Due

BROADMAN
B P
SUPPLIES

Code 4386-04, CLS-4, Broadman Supplies, Nashville, Tenn.,
Printed in U.S.A.